Corporate Reporting Practices in Public Enterprises

Corporate Reporting Practices in Public Enterprises

DR. DHANESHWAR DAMOR MEENA
(MBA., M.Com., PGDBM., Ph.D.)

Ess Ess Publications
4837/24, ANSARI ROAD, DARYA GANJ
NEW DELHI-110002
Phone : 3260807

First Published 1995

ISBN : 81-7000-189-7

Rs. 200.00

Published by
of **Ess Ess Publications**
4837/24, Ansari Road, Darya Ganj
New Delhi-110 002 Ph. 3260807

Composed by
Classic Computer Services
RZ 128/6K Lane No. 9 East Sagar Pur,
New Delhi-110 046 Ph. 5529455

Printed at Excellent Printers, B-85, Naraina Indl. Area, Phase-II, New Delhi-28.

Corporate Reporting Practices in Public Enterprises

DR. DHANESHWAR DAMOR MEENA
(MBA., M.Com., PGDBM., Ph.D.)

Ess Ess Publications
4837/24, ANSARI ROAD, DARYA GANJ
NEW DELHI-110002
Phone : 3260807

First Published 1995

ISBN : 81-7000-189-7

Rs. 200.00

Published by
of **Ess Ess Publications**
4837/24, Ansari Road, Darya Ganj
New Delhi-110 002 Ph. 3260807

Composed by
Classic Computer Services
RZ 128/6K Lane No. 9 East Sagar Pur,
New Delhi-110 046 Ph. 5529455

Printed at Excellent Printers, B-85, Naraina Indl. Area, Phase-II, New Delhi-28.

To the memory of
My noble and loving friend
S. K. Sethi

Quem di diligunt
Adolescens moritur dum valet, sentit sapit
'Whom the gods love die young, while still
they can enjoy Health, tastes and senses'

PLAUTUS

Contents

PREFACE

The growth of the state level public enterprises is the result of a combination of socio-economic and political factors. The state level public enterprises (SLPEs) have been viewed as an instrument for socio-economic development. The SLPEs consists of a variety of entities and are involved in a wide range of diversified activities. At present, SLPEs in our country are covering a wide range of socio-economic activities. Madhya Pradesh is the heart land and the largest state of India. Its economic and industrial prosperity has greater effect on Indian socio-economic development. Therefore, the central and state Governments have established a number of state enterprises in this state. As 31st Oct.,1992, there are 33 SLPEs in the state with an investment of Rs. 21,000 crores.

Corporate reporting is a means by which SLPEs can demonstrate its accountability for resources entrusted to it. It provides information necessary for users to assess the entity's stewardship, compliance with relevant authorities, state of finances, performance and economic impact. A major function of financial reporting by the MPSLPEs is to facilitate for public appraisal of their performance from the stand point of maximising the aggregate economic welfare of the society. However, the disclosure of information through annual reports has undergone vital changes from time to time. In view of requirements to give 'true and fair' view of company's states of affairs, the management is trying to disclose more and more information.

The developments are taking place in the accounting and reporting world for making the corporate report more communicative. The accounting and professional bodies and Government around the world are continuosly trying to bring changes in quantity and quality of information. With the changing environment of the society and information needs of the users of the corporate report, The corporate reporting has shifted from the traditional reporting of financial statements (profit and loss account and balance sheet) to the modern corporate reporting which not only includes the quantitative information but also wide range of qualitative information. The reporting practices of a corporate body are affected by certain enactments, recommendations of government committees, accounting standards, accounting bodies and by the management of an enterprise.

The present study deals with the evaluation of corporate reporting practices in Madhya Pradesh SLPEs. The study has been made to examine the current information disclosure practices in corporate annual report with respect to their contents, extent of disclosure, timeliness and readability. The study is based on a purposive sample of sixteen SLPEs (in case of readability 18 PEs).

The study has been divided into five chapters. The introductory chapter deals with current developments regarding the disclosure of information and research methodology of the study. The subsequent three chapters examines content analysis and, extent of disclosure, timeliness of corporate reporting and readability of corporate reports. The analysis has been made by formulating hypothesis with the independent variables and company characteristics. In the end, the major finding of the study along with suggestions to various interested agencies were narrated briefly in the fifth chapter.

It is certainly a great advantage and pleasure for me to put into words my deepest sense of gratitute and humble regards to my esteemed guide Professor NAGESHWAR RAO, Director, Pt. Jawahar Lal Nehru Institute of Business Management, Vikram University, Ujjain, who has been my source of inspiration and valuable suggestions specially I am also grateful to him for writing the foreward of this book. I am extremely greatful to the **Managing Directors** of the MPSLPEs who could provide their corporations annual reports and enabled me to complete this work successfully.

I place on record with high appreciation the encouragement and insight provided by **Dr. R.K. Jain** in the completion of this research work. I am also thankful to my Institute Librarian Dr. Kaushik Bose who has helped in so many ways in my endavour.

I am indeed thankful to my **wife Mrs. Anju Damor** for her constant encouragement and making me free from all domestic concern and extended all feasible help and comforts during the course of this project.

Last but not the least I am thankful to Mr. Sumit Sethi managing editor, ESS ESS Publications for taking special interest in publishing this work.

March, 1995.

Dhaneshwar Damor Meena
Lecturer
Pt. Jawaharlal Nehru Institute
of Business Management
Vikram University,
Ujjain.

FOREWORD

The needs of corporate report users have increased substantially. They now want at least adequate, timely and readable information. For that, we have to make the information useful, effective and relevant. The corporate reporting scenario in public enterprises is poor. The problem is much more agravated in SLPEs. The enterprises should make efforts in this direction. The issues with regards to stewardship, performance, economic impact and compliance of norms is SLPEs can only be examined through an effective system of corporate reporting. Such system facilitates the public appraisal of the performance of SlPEs for maximising the economic welfare of the society. The developments are taking place in the corporate reporting for making the contents of annual reports more relevant, adequate and communicative. The professionals are continuously making efforts to upgrade the quality and quantity of accounting information.

The book is the improved and updated volume of approved thesis of the author submitted by him to the Vikram University for the degree of Doctor of Philosphy in the Faculty of Management Studies. The author has examined the timeliness and readability of corporate reporting. In addition, fruitful analysis with respect to content analysis and extent of information disclosure has also been made. He has made carefully considered suggestions which are worthy of serious thought.

Dr. D Meena has an excellent academic and industrial background in the sphere of Financial Management. He has brought to bear upon the thesis, his excellence in an admirable manner. I regard it as a distinct honour in have been invited to present this foreword to a book which, I hope, would command a very wide readership. It would also open grounds for other researchers to venture in this field.

24-4-95

Nageshwar Rao
Professor and Director
Pt Jawaharlal Nehru
Institute of Business Management
Vikram University, Ujjain (M.P.)

List of Exhibits

List of Abbreviations

AS	Accounting Standard
BPE	Bureau of Public Enterprises
C&AG	Comptroller and Auditor General of India
CE	Capital employed
DPE	Department of Public Enterprises
ICAI	Institute of Chartered Accountants of India
ICSI	Institute of Company Secretaries of India
ICWAI	Institute of Cost and Works Accountants of India
H_o	Null Hypothesis
MPAIDC	Madhya Pradesh Agro-Industries Development Corporation
MPBCC	Madhya Pradesh Bridge Construction Corporation
MPCSC	Madhya Pradesh Civil Supplies Corporation
MPEB	Madhya Pradesh Electricity Board
MPEDC	Madhya Pradesh Energy Development Corporation
MPFC	Madhya Pradesh Financial Corporation
MPFDC	Madhya Pradesh Forest Development Corporation
MPSIDC	Madhya Pradesh State Industrial Development Corporation
MPPHC	Madhya Pradesh Police Housing Corporation
MPS&FDC	Madhya Pradesh Seeds and Farms Development Corporation
MPSED	Madhya Pradesh Electronic Development Corporation
MPSIC	Madhya Pradesh State Industrial Corporation
MPSIDC	Madhya Pradesh Small Industries Development Corporation
MPSLPEs	Madhya Pradesh State Level Public Enterprises
MPSRTC	Madhya Pradesh State Road Transport Corporation
MPTC	Madhya Pradesh Textile Corporation
PEs	Public Enterprises
SLPEs	State Level Public Enterprises

1

INTRODUCTION

Corporate reporting is the total communication system between an enterprise and users. This is the most direct, least expensive, most timely and fairest methods of reaching present and potential users. It includes not only financial statements but also other means of communicating information that relates, directly or indirectly, to the information provided by the accounting system-that is information about an enterprise's resources, obligations learnings etc. To make financial reporting effective, it must be relevant, timely, uniform and expressed in a clear language which should be free from jargons. "Companies may gain by using computers to generate reports-summarizing data, analysing them and putting them in a readable format"[1]. The usefulness of the annual report depends on the insight and interest of the audience.

1.1 Disclosure in Corporate Reports:

Disclosure can be defined[2] as a process through which a business enterprise communicates with the external parties. American Accounting Association[3] defines, disclosure "as the movement of information from private domain (i.e. inside information) into public domain". The Corporate reports are disclosed through company annual reports. This is a periodical statement[4] which is issued at the end of each accounting period. The periodical statements are prepared on the basis of generally accepted accounting principles (GAPP). The annual report usually consists of accounting information and non-accounting information.

Accounting information are quantitative , formal, structural, numerical and past oriented materials. This includes Balance sheet[5], profit and loss accounts, schedules and notes to financial statements. These are generally audited by a qualified auditor. They must exhibit "true and fair view[6]" of the state of affairs. The other accounting information are current cost accounting, human resource accounting, value added statements, financial performances of business and ratio, etc. which belong to an audited group. The non-accounting information are qualitative, narrative, unaudited and future oriented prose as per

`Statement of Accounting concepts. It usually includes Directors' reports, Chairmans' report, Accounting Policies, corporate profile and future prospects of Company etc. Non-accounting information like accounting information has impact on the investors' behaviour. The relevance of certain types of non-quantitative information can be determined by the relevance of the quantitative data to which they relate.

The presentation of annual report has undergone vital changes[7] from time to time yielding to demands of time and extent of popularity of the forms of business organisations. The environment demands for greater disclosure in the interest of various parties. As per the legal requirements, all listed companies must publish in News Papers the unaudited statement of accounts of every six months period (including current year six months and previous year six months). Due to the requirement of law and practice, the management is trying to publish more and more information.

1.2 Emerging Horizons of Corporate Reporting:

The openness in affairs of the companies is the basic principle in securing responsible behaviour. Today no enlightened management can remain aloof to the national problems. In this context, a corporation should not only be economically viable but should also pass the test of a socially responsible entity by being able to discharge its social obligations in the course of its business activities. Infact in India, the public sector companies have accepted this challenge and their Directors' report has been used to provide a meaningful background to the accounting information presented in the financial statements and for having some view of the future. The emerging horizons in Corporate reporting are discussed in brief, on the following lines:

a. Inflation Accounting:

The failure to adjust for price level changes[8] affects not only the measurement of a single division over time but also the comparision among different divisions at the same point in time. Current Cost Accounting as a method of accounting[9] for inflation has gained international recognition and a number of Dutch companies including the electronic giant Philips are preparing accounts on the basis of this method. The Research Committee of the Institute of Chartered Accountants of India in 1982 has issued a guidance note on the subject of accounting for changing prices and recommends the use of current cost accounting method. In India, companies in the private sector do not exhibit in their Annual Reports accounts showing effect of changing prices. Ashok Leyland Ltd. had exhibited in their Annual Report financial statements restated by following Current Purchasing Power Method. On the other hand, many public enterprises have restated their financial statements by following Current Cost Accounting method. A few of them are:

a. Cement Corporation of India Ltd (CCI)
b. The Minerals and Metals Trading Corporation of India Ltd (MMTC).
c. Oil and natural Gas Commission (ONGC)
d. Hindustan Aeronautics Ltd. (HAL).

b. Value Added Statement

In India, there is no statutory compulsion for incorporating value added statement in the published accounts of companies. The following corporations in India are incorporating value added statement in their Annual Reports which are exhibited for the benefit of the participants:

(i) Cement Corporation of India Ltd (CCI)
(ii) Madras Refineries Ltd (MRL)
(iii) The Minerals and Metals Trading Corporation of India Ltd (MMTC).
(iv) The Associated Cement Companies Ltd (ACC).

c. Human Resource Accounting

The balance sheet prepared on the basis of historical cost does not reflect the value of the human asset[10], since according to the current accounting practice expenditure incurred on human asset is treated as of revenue nature. Some of the methods suggested for evaluating the human assets are:

(i).Historical Cost Basis (ii).Replacement Cost Basis (iii). Present Value Method. On a general review, it is observed that most of the companies prefer to follow the third method, namely, Present Value Model. Under this method, three models are generally referred to: (i). Lev and Schwartz (ii). Flamholtz Model (iii). Jaggi lau's Model. The following public enterprises have followed Lev and Schwartz Model:

(i) Bharat Heavy Electricals Ltd (BHEL).
(ii) The Minerals and Metals Trading Corporation Ltd. (MMTC).
(iii) Madras Refiner Ltd. (MRL)
(iv) Cement Corporation India Ltd. (CCI) - this company has also followed Flamhottz model and Jaggi Lau's model.

d. Ecology Reporting

Upto the year 1985, there were no stringent laws developed for control of pollution of air and water to be enforced strictly by Governmental Agencies in India. The Environmental Protection Act was enacted in India in May 1986 pursuant to which it was imperative for all new projects to build environmental safeguards into the project at the planning stage and implement them subsequently. However, practically none of the leading companies in public and private sector have made reference in their annual reports about the steps taken for pollution control but in the next decade after the enactment of the above Act, corporations are likely to disclose effective steps taken for pollution control.

e. Social Accounting

It is observed that leading public sector companies have made efforts to bring out "social Accounts"[11] comprising social income statement and social balance sheet. The social Income Statement generally comprises of three sub statements, (i) social benefits and costs to staff (ii) social benefits and costs to community and (iii) social benefits and costs to general public. If social benefits exceed social costs under the above three sub-statements, the resultant figure is net social income to staff, community and general public". and "net social loss to staff, community and general public" in case social costs exceed social benefits. It is noted that social accounts are prepared by leading public sector companies and exhibited in their annual reports, but none of the leading private sector companies have undertaken this exercise. The annual reports of the following public enterprises have exhibited Social Accounts :

a. Cement Corporation of India Ltd (CCI).
b. Madras Refineries Ltd. (MRL).
c. The Minerals and Metals Trading Corporation Ltd. (MMTC).
d. Oil and Natural Gas Commission (ONGC).

1.3. Disclosure Requirements of Department of Public Enterprises (DPE):

The DPE[12] as a centralised body has recommended to disclose the following information in the report of Board of Directors' of central PE.

1. A summary of financial results indicating the annual turnover, profit after depreciation and interest but before tax, provision

of taxation, net profit, appropriation to reserve, proposed dividend, etc.

2. Information about increase in paid up capital, long term loans, etc.
3. Important changes in accounting policies.
4. Changes in accounting methods such as changes in depreciation method, valuation of inventories, etc.
5. Main events which have influenced the production and profitability of the company under report and out look for forthcoming years.
6. General order book position and prediction performances vis-a-vis capacities and targets.
7. Export achievement and foreign exchange earnings together with future outlook.
8. Any significant achievements in import substitution or development of new products, etc.
9. Employee-employer relations:- strikes, lockouts, incentives schemes, training, etc.
10. New projects or expansions contemplated to increase or diversify the production and progress made so far.
11. Staff welfare activities: township, education, health, facilities, etc.
12. Changes in the Board of Directors and general managers.
13. Disclosure of capital and revenue social overheads separately in annual report.

1.4 Research Methodology:

The research methodology of the present study has been narrated briefly in this section. The methodolgy consists the needs of study, objectives of the study, review of literature, scope of study, sample introduction and profile, data collection, presentation and analysis and limitations of the study.

1.4.1 Need of Study :

The new developments are taking place in the contents and extent of information disclosed in corporate reports. Besides the statutory requirements as laid down in Companies Act for profit and loss account, balance sheet, audit report, Report of Directors, the comments of comptroller and Auditor General of India, a healthy trend has emerged with many progressive companies giving additional information and data in their annual reports such as physical and financial programmes, achievement in relation to programmes, productivity, costing of production, price standard, employment trend, labour relations, organisation change, social and human resource accounting, disclosure of accounting policies of individual items in final accounts, non-financial aspects which can not strictly be justified on economic consideration and effect of such items etc. An annual report aims at providing a clear picture of the problems and achievements, a perspective for future and co-relate its achievement with those in past. However, the differences in reporting widely exist in PEs. Also there is inadequate information as per legal requirements. Present practices of corporate reporting paricularly in MPSLPEs are criticised on the following grounds :

1. Annual reports do not provide simplified and easily understandable information.
2. It does not exhibit 'true and fair facts'.
3. It does not contain sufficient information needed by parties to make their decision.
4. Level of information disclosure is not as per the legal requirements.
5. Non-financial facts and their effects not stated.
6. Reporting standard has not been improved with change of accounting principles and technological innovation etc.

Looking into the criticism of present corporate reporting, there is a need to review the 'annual reporting' mechanism. This will give an improved, more information oriented and effective mechanism of corporate reporting with a view to induce PEs to adopt a logical and perspective corporate reporting system.

1.4.2 Objects of the Study :

The main object of the study is to evaluate the corporate reporting practices of MPSLPEs so that concrete plan of action may be suggested to improve the corporate reporting practices of MPSLPEs. The objectives emanating from the main objective of the study are as follows :-

(i) To analyse the contents of corporate reports.
(ii) To examine the extent of disclosures in MPSLPEs.
(iii) To ascertain the quantum of voluntary information in MPSLPEs.

(iv) To examine the influence of company characteristics on the information disclosures trends of MPSLPEs.

(v) To identify the time lags in corporate reporting system of MPSLPEs.

(vi) To examine the influence of company characteristics on various types of time lags.

(vii) To analysis the readability trends of corporate report.

(viii) To suggest a concrete plan of action for individual PEs, BPE. Professional bodies and State Government.

1.4.3 Review of Literature :

The theoritical frame work and base for evaluation of corporate disclosure practices, timeliness of corporate report and readability of annual reports have been developed through extensive study of available literature relating to the present study. These includes accounting theory, standard text and references, International and Indian accounting standards of corporate reporting, statements of standard auditing practices, relevant provisions in Companies act 1956 relating to the requirement of disclosure in context of "true and fair view" of disclosures of information, recommendations and requirement of disclosure of information as per the statement-I, etc. The annual reports of giant central PEs and SLPEs were also referred. A number of books, Journals, magazines and related research work undertaken by others were studied. In Indian context, the research work on disclosure practices includes Dr. Jawahar Lal[13], Dr. R.C. Sharma[14], Dr. Dasgupta[15], Dr. Claire Marston[16], Dr. H.M.Damania[17]. Other studies include the work of David F.Howkins[18], Baker Mertion, Rudolf flech[19] Robert Gunnings[20]. More details regarding these studies are narrated in related chapters.

1.4.4. Scope of Study :

The study is limited to the study of information contents and its availability in the latest published annual report of selected MPSLPEs as on 31.3.90. Unpublished information and other related published information has not been considered for the purpose of the study. The aspects like contents and extent of disclosure, timeliness and readability were covered.

1.4.5 Plan of the Study

The research work has been planned within a frame work to avoid disorder and ambiguity in the process of conducting the study. The plan is also intended to provide a clearcut approach to researcher. The main objective of the research is to evaluate the corporate reporting practices of MPSLPEs so that a concrete plan of action may be suggested to improve the Corporate reporting practices of MPSLPES.The study attempts to evaluate the corporate annual reports by evaluating the three important factors of annual report. They are the extent of information disclosure,timeliness of corporate reporting and readability of corporate annual reports.

In the process of evaluation of quantity of disclosures, a base for comparing the current actual disclosure has been developed on the basis of information disclosure requirements of Companies Act, 1956, disclosure requirements of DPE, disclosure requirement of Indian Standards and voluntary disclosures. The entire content has been grouped in three groups- Directors report, Accounting information (both statutory) and voluntary information . Then actual disclosure has been compared in order to find the disclosure position. The last stage of evaluation is the examination of relationship of quality of information disclosure with company characteristics. They have been conceptualised as quantity of information (dependant variable) and company characteristics viz. Age, Turnover, Rate of turnover, Rate of return, Capital employed and Size of employment are assumed as independant variables. While examining relationship with each variable, other variables are presumed to remain constant.Similar process has been followed in examining the relationship with readability and timeliness of reports.

1.4.6. Sample Profile :

According to the annual report of Department of Public Enterprises Bhopal, there are thirty three SLPEs in M.P. state. The enterprises are grouped into Promotional, Financial, Commercial and Service enterprises. They are also classified on the basis of the incorporation statutes. A sample consisting of 18 enterprises which constitute about 54% of the universe are included in the study. For the analysis of contents and extent of disclosure and timeliness the annual reports of sixteen SLPEs were taken into account.

The introductory details of the sample is shown in exhibit No.1.1.

The sample profile of the units under study are categorised as follows :

(a) Naturewise

	No. of SLPEs
1. Commercial	11
2. Service	3
3. Financial	1
4. Promotional	3
	18

(b). On the basis of incorporation statute

Act.	No. of SLPEs
1. Companies act	11
2. Special act	5
3. Societies registration act	2
	18

(c). Turnoverwise

Turnover (Rs.lakhs)	No. of SLPEs
1-1000	8
1000-2000	2
2000-3000	4
3000-4000	0
4000-5000	1
5000 and above	3
	18

(d). Employment wise

(No. of Employees)	No. of SLPEs
100-500	5
500-1000	7
1000-1500	0
1500 and above	1
	13

(e). Age wise

Age (Years)	No. of SLPEs
1-10	6
10-20	6
20-30	4
30-40	2
	18

(f). On the basis of Capital employed

Rs. in Lakhs	No. of SLPEs
0 - 500	4
500 - 1000	5
1000- 1500	0
1500 -2000	2
2000 -2500	3
2500 -3000	0
3000 and above	4
	18

1.4.7. Data Collection :

The primary source of data for the study is the published annual report of M.P.State level public enterprises. The latest available published annual reports were collected from head offices of the corporations. ExhibitNo. 1.2 shows the details of Annual reports taken for the purpose of study. The required data were obtained from the annual reports by way of content analysis.

1.4.8. Processing and Analysis of Data :

Information collected through the content analysis of annual reports were edited for correctness, consistency and homogeneity. Then data are classified on the basis of Directors report, Accounting information and voluntary or Non-statutory information. The following aspects have been examined : (i) Extent of corporate disclosure practices (ii) Timeliness (iii) Readabililty of Corporate reports regarding the quantity and quality of disclosure in corporate annual reports of the selected MPSLPEs. The following evaluation mechanism (for timeliness and readability, refer related chapters) has been used :

EXHIBIT No. 1.1

Introductory Details of Sample Units

Name of MPSLPEs	Age (to the date of A.R.)	Employment Nos.	Profit Rs.lakhs	Turnover Rs.lakhs	Rate of Return %	Capital employed Rs.lakhs	Rate of turnover %	Paid up Share Capital lakh Rs.
1. Agro.Industries Development Corpn.	19	-	28.45	2581.13	5.05	563.07	458.40	274.50
2. Forest Development Corporation	10	833	13.76	2305.86	0.63	2199.18	104.85	698.00
3. Small Industries Development Corpn.	18	749	113.60	2361.86	20.69	549.24	430.03	281.49
4. Energy Development Corporation	6	278	-	445.04	-	68.92	646.73	68.92
5. Financial Corpn.	35	-	719.86	4443.45	12	29966.41	15.00	3636.26
6. Police Housing Corporation	8	-	(-24.90)	97.94	(-3.12)	796.88	12.29	200.00
7. Seeds & Farms Development Corpn.	9	521	41.43	1797.84	2.51	1649.43	2.51	414.20
8. Industrial Development Corporation	20	134	14.13	457.55	0.19	7468.00	6.13	7468.00
9. State Industries Corpn	24	-	(-19.87)	562.72	2.26	877.79	64.11	773.70
10. State Road Transpais Corpn	28	-	0.47	18875.00	0.01	11885.00	158.81	9320.00
11. Fisheries Dev.Corpn.	8	259	4.45	198.22	3.83	116.17	130.63	41.78
12. Electronic Dev.Corpn.	8	500	36.25	1173.48	1.49	2132.18	48.24	1741.25
13. Land Development Corpn	26	876	-	395.18	-	2470.00	-	1083.49

14. Textile Corporation	16	394	26.14	2378.80	4.09	714.06	333.13	535.95
15. Bridge Construction Corporation	7	775	(-8.40)	177.68	(-1.72)	489.35	36.31	500.00
16. Civil Supplies Corpn.	13	959	(-68.66)	21737.61	(-24.92)	275.44	7891.95	50.00
17. Electricity Board	36	100390	1252.00	127521.00	0.26	481330.00	26.49	-
18. Tourist Development Corporation	12	767	1.33	316.42	(-0.54)	1597.04	19.81	-

Source: Compiled from the Annual Reports of the concerned study units.

(a) Identification and Grouping of Items of Information:

After going through the disclosure requirements of Statutory and Non-statutory items, 215 items in total were identified for the disclosure in the annual reports of these SLPEs.

The items were classified into following three major groups:

Group	No. of Items
a. Directors report	53
b. Accounting Information	137
c. Voluntary items	25
Total	215

These items have been selected in the light of statutory provisions, disclosure practices of central PEs and disclosure standards of ICAI. Some of these items may not be applicable to individual SLPE. Hence, the total number of items relevant to an SLPE may vary widely.

EXHIBIT No.1.2

Details of Annual Report of Sample Units.

MPSLPEs	Accounting Year	Date Auditors Signature	Date C&AGs Signature	Date Annual general meeting
1. Agro Industries Development Corpn.	87-88 (30th June)	9.11.92	19.1.93	5.3.93
2. Forest Development Corporation	84-85 (30th June)	11.10.91	-	30.6.92
3. Small Industries Development Corpn.	88-89 (31th March)	21.12.91	12.3.92	30.4.92
4. Energy Development Corporation	87-88 (30th June)	31.08.90	15.4.91	5.7.91
5. Financial Corpn.	89-90 (30th March)	31.05.90	-	29.6.90
6. Police Housing Corporation	88-89 (31st March)	27.07.91	8.8.91	23.9.91
7. Seeds & Farms Development Corpn.	88-89 (31st March)	10.05.91	-	15.7.91
8. Industrial Development Corporation	84-85 (31st March)	07.08.89	-	30.3.90

9.	State Industries Corporation	84-85 (31st March)	18.11.89	-	06.1.90
10.	State Road Strns. Corporation	86-87 (31st March)	05.04.89	-	18.1.91
11.	Electronic Devel-opment Corpn.	85-86 (31st March)	07.01.92	3.2.92	25.2.92
12.	Land Development Corporation	87-88 (30th June)	12.05.89	-	7.3.90
13.	Textile Corporation	85-86 (31st Dec.)	30.04.92	9.7.92	4.8.92
14.	Bridge Constru-ction Corporation	84-85 (31st March)	29.09.86	28.11.86	22.3.86
15.	Civil Supplies Corporation	86-87 (31st March)	27.07.91	03.10.91	04.11.92
16.	M.P.E.B	88-89 (31st March)	23.9.91	-	03.11.91

Source: Compiled from the Annual Reports of the concerned units.

(b). Scoring of Items of Information:

Each item of the information has been assigned an arbitrary score on the following basis:

Items disclosed in annual report : 1

Items not disclosed in the report : 0

Items not applicable : x (Excluded)

Then, the score of each annual report is totalled under each head (Directors' report, Accounting information and Voluntary information) and aggregate as grand total. The relevent items applicable under each head and aggregate have been computed. The disclosure percentage of each annual report for each head is computed by using the following formula :

$$\text{Disclosure percentage} = \frac{\text{Total score of Individual Enterprise}}{\text{Maximum Applicable score of individual company}} \times 100$$

(c). Disclosure of Each items of Information :

Disclosure of an item of information by the enterprise included in the sample has been worked out. The enterprise which has disclosed the items is assigned the score "1". The enterprise which has not disclosed the item of information has been assigned the Zero. The disclosure percentage of each item by the sampled PEs is computed by using the following formula :

$$\text{Disclosure percent of an item} = \frac{\text{No. of SLPEs disclosing the item}}{\text{No. of SLPEs which must have disclosed the item}} \times 100$$

1.4.9. Formulation of Hypothesis:

In order to find the relationship and effects of the company characteristics on the quantity of information disclosure in annual reports, timeliness of corporate disclosure and quality of readability of annual report of MPSLPEs, a total of sixty eight null hypotheses have been formulated and tested. In addition, one hypothesis on timeliness was formulated in the context of statutory period allowed for the release of annual reports. The number of null hypotheses formulated and tested and in each chapter and in its subheads have been shown in exhibit No. 1.3.

EXHIBIT No. 1.3

Chapterwise and Segmentwise Classification of Formulated Null Hypotheses

S.N.	Chapter	Segments	Null Hypotheses: From	Null Hypotheses: To	Numbers of Null Hypothesis tested
1.	Extent of Information Disclosures (Quantity of information (Chapter-2).	(i) Directors report	H^1_0	H^5_0	5
		(ii) Accounting information	H^6_0	H^{10}_0	5
		(iii) Voluntary information	H_0^{11}	H^{15}_0	5
		(iv) Aggregate	H^{16}_0	H^{20}_0	5
		Subtotal			20
2.	Timelines in Corporate reporting (Chapter-3).	(i) Total time lag	H^{21}_0	H^{26}_0	6
		(ii) Audit lag	H^{27}_0	H^{32}_0	6
		(iii) C & AG's lag	H^{33}_0	H^{38}_0	6
		(iv) Reporting lag	H^{39}_0	H^{44}_0	6
		Subtotal			24
3.	Readability of corportate reports	(i) Readability of Corporate report	H^{45}_0	H^{50}_0	6
		(ii) Readability of Directors report	H^{51}_0	H^{56}_0	6
		(iii) Readability of Auditors report	H^{57}_0	H^{62}_0	6

Chapter-4).	(iv) Readibility of Footnotes & Notes Account.	H^{63}_0	H^{68}_0	6
	Subtotal			24
	Grand total			68

Source: Compiled from the details of analysis of related chapters.

1.4.10. Use of Statistical Tools:

In the process of analysis, the statistical tools of mean, range, co-efficient of variation, standard deviation, co-efficient of correlation and index numbers were used. For testing the hypothesis, the "t" test was used. The tools used and their formula are as follows :

(i) The formula for computation of the mean is as follows:

$$X = \frac{\varepsilon x}{N}$$

Where x = Arithmetic mean

ε x = Sum of all value of the variable x

N = Number of observations

(ii) In order to determine the reliablity of mean, to compare the series of two variables with regards to their variability, to facilitate the use of correlation analysis and testing of the hypotheses, the following measures of dispersion have been used:

(a). Range and Co-efficient of Range :

(i) R = L - S

(ii) $\text{Coefficient of Ranges} = \frac{L - S}{L + S}$

Where R = Range
L = Largest value of an Item
S = Smallest value of an Item

(b). Standard deviation and Coefficient of Variations :

$$\sigma = \frac{(\Sigma (x - X)^2)^{1/2}}{(N)^{1/2}}$$

σ = Standard deviation

$\Sigma (x - X)^2$ = Sum of deviations of all value from the mean

N = No. of observations

x = Value of individual observations

X = Arithmetic mean

$$\text{Coefficient of Variation} = \frac{\sigma}{X} \times 100$$

(iii) To determine the degree of relationship between two variables testing of their significance and establishing the cause and effect (if any) relationship, the Karl Pearsons' coefficient of correlation is used. The formula is as follows :

(a)
$$r = \frac{N\Sigma XY - (\Sigma X)(\Sigma Y)}{(N\Sigma X^2 - (\Sigma X)^2)^{1/2} \; (N\Sigma Y^2 - (\Sigma Y)^2)^{1/2}}$$

Where

r = Coefficient of correlation

N = Number of observations

X and Y = Variables

(b) In order to test the significance of an observed coefficient of correlation between two variables, the students "t" distribution test has been used. The formula of "t" test is as follows :

$$t = \frac{r}{(1 - r^2)^{1/2}} \times (N - 2)^{1/2}$$

Here, "t" is based on (n-2) degrees of freedom.

(c). The "t" test has been also used for testing the significance of mean in timeliness of corporate disclosure. The formula is as follows :

$$= \frac{(X - u)\,(n)^{1/2}}{S}$$

Here X = Actual mean of samples

u = Hypothetical mean

S = Standard deviation

n = Sample size.

(IV) Percentage or index :

The percentage or index method of data analysis has been used to bring the divergent data at common base. Some percentages are also calculated to compare them for relative studies.

1.4.11 Limitations of Study :

The study is aimed to examine the state of corporate reporting practices of MPSLPEs at a particular point of time. The findings of this study may not be relevant to SLPEs in other states or central PEs'. No attempt has been made to study the trend of disclosure practices. The study is based only on the published data at a particular point of time. The reports for particular year or uniform year are not available. Hence we have considered only the latest report available for these SLPEs as on 31 March 1990. We could not give an appropriate model of corporate reporting mechanism for MPSLPEs as almost all of them are not even meeting the bare minimum statutory requirements.

REFERENCES

1. Richman, D. J. Thescon, M.H. Bovel, C.L. Thill, J.V. *Business Today* M.c graw Publishing Co. New York, 1990, p.403.
2. Jawahar Lal *Corporate Annual Report Theory & Practice,* Sterling Publishers Private Limited, New Delhi, 1985, p.38.
3. American Accounting Association. *Conceptual framework for Financial Accounting and Reporting: Elements of Financial Statement and Their Measurement*, AAA June 1977, p.19.
4. Himstreet, W.C. Berly, W.M, *Business Communications* Wads Worth Publishing Co. Inc. California 1973, pp. 357-380 (guide lines for writing the reports effectively).
5. For the purpose of analysis, refer Bhattacharya, H *How to Read a balance Sheet,* Oxford & IBH Publishing Co. Pvt. LTD New Delhi, 1991.
6. Rao, C.R. *Balance Sheets How true and How Fair* Brahmi Publishers, Bangalore, 1991 p.18.
7. For detailed study of words, sentences, fundamentals of report writing, graphical aids to communication, refer, Lesikar, R.V. *Basic Business Communication*, Richard D.Irvin Inc. Hovewool, illinnois 1979.
8. Illustrative example in Kaplan, R.S. and Atkinson, A.A. *Advanced Management Accounting* Preintice-Hall of India Pvt.LTD, New Delhi, 1990, pp. 669-691.
9. Horngren, CT and Suden, G.L, *Introduction to Management Accounting* Preintice-Hall of India LTD, New Delhi, 1990, p.763.
10. For elementary idea about HRA, refer, Arunachalam, M.A.S. Raman K.S. *Advanced Accountancy* Himalya Publishing House, 1991, pp.526-532

11. Claire Maston *Financial Reporting in India* Croom Helm Publishers, London 1986, p.95.

12. BPE/10 (1) Adv (1) 1968 dt. 11 September, 1968, Circular No. BPE-8(1) F/67 18 Sep 1967, No. BPE (1) 17, Adv (f)/69 dt 5 March 1969.

13. Jawaharlal, *Corporate Annual reports: Theory and Practice* opcited p.103-191.

14. R.C. Sharma, *Financial Reporting in Public Enterprises*, Tiwari Publishers, Delhi - 1991.

15. Das Gupta, *Financial Reporting in India*, Sultan Chand & Sons,1977.

16. Claire Marston, *Financial Reporting in India*,Crown Helm,London,1986

17. H.M. Damania, *"Corporate Financial Reporting in India"* The Chartered Accountant, Vol. XXXVIII - 5 Nov, 1989, p.405.

18. David F. Howkins, *Corporate Financial Reporting - Text and Cases*,Richard D.Irvin,Inc.Homewood illonois 1988.

19. Rudolf Flesch, "*How to test Readability*" Harper & brothers, New York, 1951, p.6.

20. Robert Gunnings," *Techniques of clear writing*" Mc Graw Hill Inc.,New York, 1952, pp.36-39.

2

CONTENT ANALYSIS AND EXTENT OF INFORMATION DISCLOSURE

The corporate annual report is the main instrument used by corporate bodies to communicate information about their state of affairs to the parties having reasonable interest[1]. Traditionally, Profit and Loss account and Balance sheet are being disclosed through annual reports. However, the disclosure of information through corporate annual reports have undergone vital changes from time to time[2]. The evolution of more complex corporate structures, new form of financing, changes in tax policies, new laws governing the industrial and commercial activities, innovation and advancement of technology, call of ecological and environmental balances[3], developments of advanced accounting concepts and principles, accounting and reporting standard, changing attitute of the society have demanded more information, higher standard of presentation and reliable economic measurements of resources and performance of the reporting entity. DAVID F HOWKINS[4] has rightly stated that "the corporate report does not rest on one generally accepted theory of accounting, rather financial decisions reflect a number of basic conventions which are more or less commonly accepted as a useful guide for selecting appropriate accounting policies. These conventions have grown out of experiences of the accountants and business executives to measure and communicate the results of operations and financial conditions of corporation as well as theoritical work of accounting scholers. In practice, accounting conventions seems to be unilateral. Their degree of acceptance stems from their usefulness to those making decisions involving accounting data.

2.1 Contents in Corporate Reports :

The contents of annual report depend upon a number of factors[5]. Besides the size, nature and activities of an enterprise, there are statutory provisions influencing the contents and its quality and quantity of information in a corporate annual report. They are mainly from (i) Companies Act, 1956 (ii) Stock Exchange Regulation Act. (iii)

Government policies and guidelines (iv). Special Acts governing the corporations (v) the policies and regulations of Department of Public Enterprises (vi) Indian and International Accounting Standards (vii) Developments in Accounting theory, conventions and concepts (viii) Managements' disclosure policies and reporting expertise[6]. These factors may have substantial impact on the contents of an annual report. The Companies Act, 1956 requires that every profit and loss account must give a "true and fair" view of the state of affairs and profit and loss account respectively. This requirement overrides the requirments of the schedule VI Pt I, II and III of Companies Act 1956 and the other relevant acts requirement concerning the matters to be included in a companies financial statements and notes on accounts. Therefore, the management and accountants provides the additional information to company with "true and fair view" requirements. These additional information disclosures has been recommended and some of these have been made mandatory by certain enactments. Therefore, the contents of annual report can be grouped as follows :

(A) Accounting Information :

They are mainly quantitative information. This type of information can be further divided into two groups as follows :

(i) Statutory Accounting Information.
(ii) Non-statutory Accounting Information.

(B) Non-accounting (Descriptive) information :

(i) Statutory non-accounting information.
(ii) Non-statutory non-accounting information.

The contents of annual report can also be classified on the following basis:

(i) Directors' report.
(ii) Accounting information.
(iii) Voluntary information.

2.2 Analysis of Contents of Corporate Annual Report of MPSLPEs:

In this section, an attempt has been made to examine the contents of annual reports of selected MPSLPEs.

2.2.1. Size and Content :

The size of annual report varies between 29 pages [MPEDC] to 143 pages (MPIDC). Size of the other reports varies between these two extremes. The contents of the report are quantitative as well as non-quantitive. The quantitative information is mostly contained in Profit and Loss Account, Balance sheet, schedules and annexures. The non-quantitative information is contained mostly in Directors' report, Auditors' report, Comment of C & AGs, Chairman statement, foot notes and notes on account and annexures. The descriptive information is also found as general information like Board of Directors notice for annual general meeting.

2.2.2. General Non-quantitative Information :

The description information in the corporate annual report includes as follows :

(a). Board of Directors :

The information in this portion of the corporate report includes the name, designation, functional area and tenure of the Directors. All MPSLPEs disclose this kind of information. The MPFC prints coloured photographs of Board of Directors. This type of information is shown in the initial pages of the reports.

(b). Registerd office, its address and Office network.

MPFC has disclosed the name and designation of field officers. The MPEB, MIDC and MPFC disclose the branch offices and their addresses.

(c). Notice :

The SLPEs have disclosed the notice of annual general meeting to share holders. It shows the date, time and place of annual general meeting., It also includes matters to be discussed in the meeting, rule and form of appointing the proxy, etc. Except MPEB, MPS & FDC, the annual reports of all other sampled units include this kind of information.

(d). Pictoral and Graphic Presentation of Data :

While going through the corporate annual report of the PEs, it is found that only few MPSLPEs' publish the data through graphs and pictures. The MPEB publish photographs of power projects, bar graphs for capacity and capacity utilized, pie charts represents the catagory and percentage of consumers, organization charts and Map of M.P. showing the location of each power project and regional offices network. The MPFC shows industry wise loan sanction and disbursed by pictorial presentation. It also publishes the M.P. state map showing the backward districts, growth centres, advanced districts and photographs of the industries assisted for modernisation and quality control schemes. The MPEDC has published the photographs of wind mills and solar systems newly developed.

2.2.3 Board of Directors' Reports :

The size of Directors' Reports of selected MPSLPEs varies between 2 and 14 pages. The corporate reports of MPCSC and MPS & FDC have Directors report of 2 pages. Incase of MPFC, its size is 14 pages. MPSEDC, MPCSC, MPEB, MPFDC have also attached annexures to the Directors report. The MPSEDC attaches an annexure to the report for providing detailed information relating to the material changes and commitments affecting the financial position of the corporation which has occured between the date of report and balance sheet date. It has also attached another annexure for providing the detailed information about energy conservation, technological absorption and foreign exchange earnings and out go. The MPFDC, MPSIC and MPCSC have annexured the report for providing the details of employees under section 217 (2a) of the Companies Act 1956. The contents of Directors report differs in nature and quantity from one enterprise to another. The Directors' report have been examined under the following heads :

Financial Matters :

The MPSLPEs disclose the following information relating to the financial matters :

(a) Operating results : Turnover achieved during the year, changes in turnover in comparison to previous year, profit earned, percentage change over previous year of profits, loss suffered and profit and loss appropriation are shown in the Directors' Report in many of the MPSLPEs. The MPPHC has disclosed provision for depreciation, depreciation charged, amount of the contract work, accumulated losses, etc. MPEDC has disclosed the turnover both of current and previous years. MPSIC and MPIDC have disclosed the profit earned or loss suffered, turnover and sales by each unit of production.

(b). Capital structure : The SLPEs have disclosed the information relating to composition of their capital. The MPSEDC has disclosed the names of shareholders, number of shares held by each shareholder and total amount of shares held by each shareholders. The details are as follows:

	Shareholder	No. of Share
1.	For and on behalf of the Govt. of Madhya Pradesh. Shri R.P.Sharma. Ex. Industries Commissioner.	5
2.	For and on behalf of the Govt. of Madhya Pradesh. Shri H.K.Meena Ex. Dy. Secretary Commerce and Industries Dept.	5
3.	For and on behalf of the Govt. of Madhya Pradesh. Shri L.K.Joshi Ex Managing Director MPAVN Ltd.	1
4.	Shri B.D. Khurana Managing Director, MPSEDC Ltd.	1
5.	In the name of Ho'ble Governor of M.P.	17,41,238
		17,41,250

MPPHC discloses the capital structure, loan from HUDCO and Government. MPFC has shown the capital structure classifying into ordinary capital, special capital loan in lieu of share capital, refinances, bonds and rate of interest on bonds and total amount. The other reports show total amount of capital structure with break-up into its segments.

Operational Activities :

The operational activities of individual PE may differ from one another depending upon the nature of business of the individual PE. The MPFC has disclosed its operational activities as loan operations giving the details of types of loans, loan sanctioned, loans disbursed in comparison to previous years, total application received for each kind of loan, amount recovered, areawise, industries segmentwise and size wise distribution of loans. It also gives the information about the promotion of new industry giving the details of area, industry and amount granted and disbursed to such industry. The MPPHC has disclosed the HUDCO plans, giving the details about the number of houses constructed, houses under construction and plans of contruction in future. The MPFDC has disclosed the information about its operational activities giving the information in brief about the plantation of different kind of trees, plantation programmes, implemented and results achieved for different kind of projects of tree plantation of various kinds of trees at different area and the agencies through which this task could be achieved. MPSAIDC disclosed the information relating to the various agriculture appliances and their spare parts produced and sold to the farmers of the MP State, quantity of insecticides produced and sold during the year. The MPS & FDC has disclosed the data relating to crops production of various kind of foodgrains during the year in each zone of the state. The MPSEDC has disclosed the quantity of production of each kind of electronic goods and the product mix. The MPSRTC has disclosed the average number of vehicles held average number of vehicle were on road and route, and Kilometres covered during the year. It also gives the number of operating depots, average expenditure per Kilometre, number of accidents per Kilometre and passenger Kilometre operated. The MPEB gives information about established production capacity and actual production (in K.W.H.) by each power project. It also provides the information regarding the supply of electricity for commercial, industrial, agriculture, domestic street, water supplies and customers. The MPCSC disclose detailed data relating to supply of food grains in the state.

Sales and Marketing :

The manufacturing and commercial MPSLPEs have disclosed the sales and marketing activities. These includes MPSIDC, MPAIDC, MPEB and MPFDC. The MPSIC has disclosed its selling medias; i.e. sales through cooperative societies, sales through its branches. It also has disclosed the quality development programmes.

Research and Development :

A few MPSLPEs have disclosed their research and development programmes. MPFIDC disclosed the quality development and consultancy services relating to new developments, MPFC has disclosed the new project development and promotion of new industries. The MPSEDC has disclosed the new products and projects taken over by the corporation during the year.

Personnel :

The MPSLPEs disclose the information by attaching an annexure to the Directors reports and giving the particulars of employees as required under section 217(a) of companies Act, 1956. MPIDC has disclosed the information about the welfare activities as housing loan facilities, childern education allowance, housing, subsidised canteen facilities. MPBCC disclosed information about employees welfare plans, payment of gratuity, bonus and insurance schemes. The MPEB has disclosed the detailed information about the personnel i.e. total number of employees in each grade pay scales, training and development.

Future Prospects :

MPPHC has mentioned in brief about the future plans of house constructions of various catagories of houses at various places in the state. The MPFDC has disclosed the information of future plans of activities of state Government for plantation of trees in next seven years. The report says that the plan covers the number of trees to be planted in different areas of the state.

Organisation and Management :

The SLPES have disclosed the information relating to organisation and management of the corporation. The information disclosed includes the appointments of Directors, composition of Committees, tenure of each Director etc. The MPFC has disclosed the name of each Director, their tenure, composition of executive committee, recovery committee, loan sanction and disbursement committee and number of meetings held during the year. MPFC, MPIDC, MPBCC, MPSEDC, MPFDC and MPEDC and MPEB also disclose the information regarding appointments and tenure of Directors.

Details of Material Changes and Commitments :

The details of materials changes and commitments affecting the financial position of the coporation which have occured from the date of balance sheet and upto the date of report as required under section 217(1) (d) of the companies Act 1956 have been disclosed by the MPSEDC. The corporation has disclosed the changes in the capital structure, change in production division, changes in communication system, new development, process, development of new projects and industry promotion. It also comments about the impact of the development on the financial position.

View of Directors Audit Report and Comments :

Directors' reports have disclosed the comments of auditors and comments of the managements against the observations and objections of audit. This has been presented by some PEs by way of an annexure to the Director report. MPEDC (Urja) has disclosed by an annexure to Directors report the comments of auditors and their settlement comments by management. It has also mentioned the audit fees and expenses incurred in this connection. MPFDC gives the name of auditors, their appointments, addresses and the year of appointment. The MPPHC, MPSIC, MPEDC, MPBCC and MPIDC have disclosed similar type of information.

Comments of the Comptroller and Auditor General :

The SLPEs disclose the comments of C & AGs through the Directors reports. The MPEDC has attached the comments of C & AGs by way of an annexure. The C & AGs comments on profit and loss, Balance sheet and the management's comments against the observation on account and audit report have been disclosed by MPEDC and MPIDC similarly.

Information About Subsidiary Company :

MPSEDC, MPIDC, MPSIDC disclose the information relating to their subsidiaries. The MPSEDC has disclosed the profit and loss account, balance of its subsidiary (Optel). It gives details of capital structure, operations results, offices, and number of employees. The MPSIC also disclose its provisional Balance sheet, Profit and Loss accounts and statement of grant utilisation for the year. MPSIDC disclose the profit and loss account, Balance sheet and gives the details about the operation results for each subsidiary.

Legal Notices and the Revival of Sick Units :

The MPFC disclosed this kind of information in the Directors report, MPFC has disclosed the number of cases pending in court for court decision, cases trial and decision given by court, amount recovered from the borrowers as a result of court decision and number of cases filed during the year. MPFC also disclose the information about the sick units such as granted loan, pending recoveries and number of such units have been granted rehabilation and renewal loan.

Information as Per Section 217 (1) (b) of Companies Act 1956.

Information under this section has been disclosed by MPSEDC Other companies do not disclose this kind of information. The MPSEDC has disclosed the information relating to power and fuel consumption giving the details of quantity purchased, quantity generated internally, and consumption relating to Research and Development specifying the area in which research and development has been carried out by the enterprise benifits derived as a result of R &D, expenditure on R & D during the financial year etc. It also discloses the information relating to technology absorption, adaptation and innovation, efforts made toward technology and adaptation and benefits derived as result of the efforts. It has also disclosed the information in respect of imported technology.

Other Information :

Some of the Directors' reports of selected MPSLPEs provide the information regarding effect of the product and plants on environment (MPEDC), high lights of the year (MPSFDC), segmental information (MPIDC), Segments profit, assets in segment, joint sectors , project, etc,.

Government Relation :

The relationship with government has been expressed by way of acknowledgement for the works done in favour of MPSLPEs.

Accounting Policies :

A few of the PES under study have disclosed the acccounting policies separately. Some of them have merged with notes on accounts. The MPSEDC have disclosed the accounting policies by way of a "statement on accounting policies". It discloses accounting policies relating to methods of depreciation , valuation of inventories, valuation of stores, policies relating to conversion of foreign currency, policies on design and treatment of prototype capital items. The MPSIC has disclosed the policies of treatment of increased salary, wages and dearness allowance. Provision for Bonus, policy of sales recognition, policies of loan recovery, accounting policy of cash system accounting, treatment of income and expenditure. MPEDC has disclosed policies for depreciation method (written down value), basis of treatment of interest, deposits (cash base) and valuation of stores.

2.2.4. Profit and Loss Account :

The MPSLPES have presented their profit and loss account either in 'T' form or in statement form. The profit and loss appropriation account form a part of profit and loss account. The detailed information about an item of profit and loss account has been provided by way of schedules. It forms part of profit and loss account. On the other hand MPFC has presented its profit and loss account in three pages without showing schedules separately. The MPPHC, MPS & FDC, MPIDC, MPCSC, MPEDC have presented their profit and loss account in "T" form. The number of schedules varies from one SLPE to another. The MPSEDC provides 14 schedules to its profit and loss account whereas MDEDC provides 4 Schedules to its profit and loss account. The MPSIDC (S) has presented its profit and loss account in a statement form and provides the details of all the items of the profit and loss account by way of eleven schedules.

The MPIDC disclose profit and loss account of each segment unit separately and also prepare a consolidated profit and loss account. Details of each item relating to segment units have been shown by way of schedules. Notes on accounts which are forming part of profit and loss account give explanation about the treatment of items in the profit and loss account. Rate of depreciation charged, provision for depreciation, Directors' remuneration, audit fees, bad debt written off, income from other sources, etc, have been shown by way of foot notes and notes on accounts. Accounting policies relating to stock valuation, material issues pricing methods, treatment of expenditures, etc., has also been shown seprately.

2.2.5 Balance Sheet :

Balance sheet has been presented either in "T" form or in vertical form. The MPSLPEs which are presenting "T" form are MPFC, MPPHC, MPFDC, MPCSC, MPEDC. The MPSLPEs which present in vertical form includes MPSEDC, MPSIDC(s), MPS&FDC, MPAIDC, etc. The schedules to the balance sheet varies between 5 and 16 in number. The schedules provides detailed information about an item appearing in balance sheet.

2.2.6 Notes on Accounts :

Notes on account varies in number and size in MPSLPEs. The MPCSC shows 36 notes on account covering 5 pages wheras MPEDCS gave 7 notes on account covering two pages, MPFDC gives 25 notes on account covering two pages. MPFDC gives 25 notes on account covering 7 pages. It gives the statistical data by way of tables in notes on account. The disclosure position of notes on account by MPSLPEs has been shown in exhibit No.3.1.

It is found that some MPSLPEs have given small notes on account with precious information whreas some MPSLPEs have given detailed information about the accounting methods, treatment of expenses etc.

EXHIBIT No. 2.1

Disclosure of Notes on Accounts and their Length

NAME OFMPSLPE	NO. OF NOTES	PAGES
MPSEDC	17	5
MPSIDC	26	3
MPIDC	14	4
MPEDC	7	2
MPFC	14	3
MPBCC	33	5
MPTC	25	5
MPCSC	36	5
MPSIDC	11	2
MPFDC	25	7
MPAIDC	14	5
MPPHC	15	2
MPS & FDC	-	-
MPEB	-	-

Source : Compiled from the Annual report of selected MPSLPEs.

2.2.7 Contingent Liabilities

A few MPSLPES have disclosed the contingent liabilities through the notes on account in their annual report. The MPSLPES which have disclosed the contingent liabilities includes MPSIC, MPSIDC, MPFDC and MPSEDC. The MPSEDC, have disclosed the contingent liabilities relating to out standing Bank guarantees, outstanding letter of credit, indeminities for advance payments, claims of central Government, excise department and for outstanding bonds for custom duty.

2.2.6 Other Additional Information Disclosures

Some MPSLPES disclose additional information which is not mandatory but it is disclosed for making corporate report more communicative . These are as follows:

(i) Accounting Ratios:

It is found that only two MPSLPEs have disclosed the ratios. Occupancy ratio has been disclosed by MPSRTC, and debt equity ratio has been disclosed by MPFDC.

(ii) Historical Summaries:

Historical summaries of financial and operational statistics have been disclosed in annual reports by MPIDC,MPFC,MPEB,MPFDC, MPEDC. MPFC disclose the loan santioned and disbursed since inception. MPFDC provides data of raw materials inventory, turnover and profit for last three years.

(iii) Funds Flow Statement :

Funds flow statements have been disclosed by MPFC, MPEB, MPSRTC and MPFDC. Others SLPES have not disclosed.

(iv) Corporate Objectives:

MPS & FDC, MPFC have disclosed the objectives of the organisation (in short).

The cash flow statement, ratios relating to liquidity and profitability, human resource accounting and value added statement have not been disclosed by any of the MPSLPEs.

2.3 Extent of Disclousure :

In this section, an attempt has been made to assess the quantity of information disclosed in the corporate annual reports of selected MPSLPES. The following steps have been taken in this regard :

2.3.1. Disclosure in Individual Corporate Report

The quantity of information disclosed in a Corporate report has been computed by using the disclosure percentage formula which is as follows:

$$\text{Disclosure percentage} = \frac{\text{Total score of Individual Enterprise}}{\text{Maximum applicable score of individual enterprise}} \times 100$$

The disclosure Percentage of each annual report and its subheads (They are Directors report, Accounting and Voluntary information) have been computed. The disclosure position of each corporate report as well as its subheads have been shown in exhibit No. 2.2.

The exhibit portrays the following disclosure position of individual annual report and its three major segments of the report.

(i) The exhibit shows that there is one MPSLPEwhich disclose between 30 and 40 percent information. The disclosure percentage of the M.P. Seeds and Farms development Corporation's is 39.62.

EXHIBIT No. 2.2

Disclosure Position of Individual Corporate Report and its Segments.

Disclosure percentage	Directors report		Accounting information		Voluntary information		Cororate report (Aggregate)	
	No. of Cos.	%	No. of Cos.	%	No. of Cos.	%	No. of Cos.	%
0-10	.	.	.	.	.	.	.	.
10-20	.	.	.	.	1	6.25	.	.
20-30	.	.	.	.	4	25.00	.	.
30-40	1	6.25	.	.	4	25.00	1	6.25
40-50	2	12.50	1	6.25	2	12.50	.	.
50-60	3	18.75	.	.	2	12.50	.	.
60-70	2	12.50	.	.	2	12.50	5	31.25
70-80	2	12.50	2	12.50	1	6.25	4	25.00
80-90	5	31.25	8	50.00	.	.	4	25.00
90-100	1	6.25	5	31.25	.	.	2	12.50

Source : Computed from the figures available in the anual reports of selected MPSLPEs.

(ii) There are 93.75% MPSLPEs.which disclose more than 60 percent information in their annual reports. There are 37.50% MPSLPEs. whose disclosure percentage is above 80%. Only 12.50% of MPSLPEs are disclosing more than 90 percent information in their annual reports.

(iii) The information disclosure in Directors report by MPSLPEs is found between 30 and 100 percent. There are 82.1% of MPSLPEs which disclose more than 50% information . 31.25% of MPSLPEs disclose 80% to 90% information . There is only one PE which disclose more than 90% information in its Directors report.

(iv) The smallest disclosure percentage in Directors report is found at 39.15% and highest disclosure is found at 97.62%. This shows wide variations in disclosure pratices.

(v) There is one MPSLPE which discloses 41% of accounting information in its annual report . The disclosure percentage of accounting information in MPSLPEs varies between 41% and 100%.

(vi) 93.25% of MPSLPEs disclose more than 70% of the accounting information. 50% of MPSLPEs disclose more than 80% and 31% of MPSLPEs disclose information ranging between 90% to 100%.

(vii) The disclosure percentage of voluntary information varies between 16% and 72% . The 68.5% of MPSLPEs disclose less then 50% and 56.25% of MPSLPEs disclose less than 40 % of voluntary information.

(viii) The exhibit clearly stresses that the disclosure of accounting information is better than other two segments.

2.3.2 Average Disclosure

The average quantity of information disclosed by the MPSLPEs in their annual reports has been calculated to obtain a single representative information disclosure of the sample. The average quantity of disclosures has been obtained for annual report as a whole and Directors' report, accounting information and voluntary information separately. The average, standard deviation from the mean, co-efficient of variation, range, co-efficient of range and variation position of the segments have been shown in exhibit No. 2.3.

The exhibit shows that there is significant variations among disclosure prectices in MPSLPEs. The following observations have been drawn from the mean disclosures and measures of dispersion :

(i) The average disclosure percentage of annual reports is 74.16%.Incase of standard deviation it is 13.84. The level varies between 39.62% and 93.12% None of MPSLPEs discloses 100% of information in its annual report. The range shows wide variations in disclosure practices of MPSLPEs.

(ii) Average disclosure (74.16 %) of annual reports shows the greater scope of improvement in corporate disclosure practices.

(iii) The average disclosure of information in Directors' report at 68.04 % reflects the attitude of MPSLPEs toward non compliance of legal provisions regarding information disclosure.

(iv) The standard deviation 16.79, co-efficient of variation 24.68% smallest disclosure 39.15% and largest disclosure 97.62% of directors reports of MPSLPEs shows wide variation among the disclosure practices in Directors' report. It also indicates that,the management of MPSLPEs does not disclose much of the statutory information.

EXHIBIT No. 2.3

Disclosure Position of the Sample

Parameters	Directors reports	Accounting information	Voluntary information	Aggregate (Annual Report)
Mean disclosure (-) %	68.04	82.92	40.25	74.16
Statndard deviation ( )	16.79	12.70	16.45	13.84
Coefficient of Range	24.68	15.70	40.86	18.66
Smallest Disclosure	39.15	41.00	16.00	39.62
Largest disclosure (%)	97.62	100.00	72.00	93.12
Coefficient of range	0.4275	0.4184	0.6364	0.4030
Order of information disclosure	III	I	IV	II
Uniformity in distribution	III	I	IV	II
Variation in distribution	II	VI	I	III

Source : Computed from the figures shown in the annual reports of selected MPSLPEs.

(v) The average disclosure of accounting information in annual reports is found at 82.92%. The smallest disclosure level is 41.00% and the largest disclosure level is 100%. The range shows high degree of variation among disclosures in MPSLPEs. However, the average disclosure of 82.92% shows a satisfactory disclosure position of accounting information.

(vi) In accounting information ,the standard deviation at 15.20 is comparatively less than the other two heads. It shows more uniform disclosures in MPSLPEs.

(vii) The average disclosure of 40.25% in case of voluntary information shows poor level of disclosure. This also shows that the lack of management vision in corporate reporting. The management's attitude towards statutory and voluntary information is also not aggresive.It has more or less limited to the legal disclosure requirements

(viii) The largest disclosure of 72%, the smallest disclosure of 16% and standard deviation of 16.45 with respect to voluntary disclosure shows high degree of variation.

(ix) The average disclosure percentage of the Directors' report (68.47%),accounting information (82.92%) and voluntary information (40.25%) shows that the disclosures of accounting information is better than the Directors' reports and Voluntary disclosures.

(x) The co-efficient of variations of Directors report (24.68), accounting information (15.70) and Voluntary information (40.86) have shown wide variations.

(xi) On examination of information disclosures of individual corporate reports it is found that the highest disclosure is 97.62% in Directors' report. 100% in accounting information and 72% in voluntary information disclosure.

(xii) It can be concluded from the above analysis that the over all disclosures in corporate reports of MPSLPEs is not satisfactory.

2.3.3 Disclosure of Individual Items:

The disclosure of individual items of information in annual reports of MPSLPES has been examined in this subsection. The number of public enterprises which have disclosed an item of information have been shown as disclosure percentage of that item. The disclosure percentage of each item of information appearing in Directors' report, Profit and Loss account and Balance sheet (accounting information) and items described as voluntary has been computed by using a formula. It is as follows:

$$\text{Disclosure percent of an item} = \frac{\text{No. of SLPEs disclosing the item}}{\text{No. of SLPEs which must have disclosed the item}} \times 100$$

The disclosure percentage of individual items of information has been shown in exhibit No. 2.4. The exhibit indicates the following disclosure position of the items :

(i) The disclosure of individual items varies between zero and hundred. 92 items (42.79%) have been disclosed by 90% to 100% companies. 31 items (14.42%) have been disclosed by 80% to 90% companies and 19 items (8.84%) have been disclosed by 70% to 80% companies. Hence 142 items (65.25%) have been disclosed by more than 70% companies.

(ii) 54 items (25.23%) have been disclosed by 0 to 50% companies and 161 (74.77%) items have been disclosed by 50% to 100% companies. The aggregate picture shows that the management of some companies ignores the disclosure of some items of information in their annual reports.

(iii) Directors reports of MPSLPES shows wide variation in disclosure percentage of individal items. 26.42% of items have been disclosed by 90% to 100% companies. There are 60.70% items which have been disclosed by more than 70% companies.

(iv) 30.19% items have been disclosed by 0% to 50 % companies and 69.81% items have been disclosed 50% to 100% companies.

(v) Disclosures of items appearing in accounting shows an increasing trend from the level of 50% disclosure. 55.47% of items have been disclosed by 90% to 100%. There are 15.33% of items which have been disclosed by 80% to 90% of Companies.

(vi) 15.31% items have been disclosed by 0 to 50% companies and 84.69% items have been disclosed by 50% to 100 % companies. It indicates a satisfactory trend of accounting information disclosure.

(vii) Voluntary items have also been disclosed by few companies. There 28.0% items which have been disclosed by 10.20% companies and there are only 8% items which have been disclosed by 90% to 100% companies.

(viii) 68% Voluntary items have been disclosed by 0-50% companies and 32% items have been disclosed by 50% to 100% companies. It indicates that the greater number of MPSLPEs disclose only a few items.

(ix) Items of Directors report (30.19%) accounting information (15.31%) and Voluntary information (68%) have disclosure percentage between 0% to 50%. Thus it shows that maximum of voluntary items have been ignored. Only a few of them are disclosed by a few companies. On the other hand, statutory items in Directors' report and accounting information have been taken into account by maximum number of companies. However, some of items of statutory nature have been ignored by a few companies.

2.4 Company Characterstics and Extent of Disclosure:

The quality and quantity of information disclosure in corporate annual report and its segments viz. Directors' Report, Accounting information and voluntary information may be affected by a number of variables of the company. Here, an attempt has been made to examine the relationship with the impact of company characteristics on extent of information disclosure. The company variables and their relationship with the quality of disclosure of information have been examined as follows:

(i) Age:

As the enterprise grows older its size of business, accounting and reporting expertise increases. Therefore, the older firm would disclose more quantity of information in their annual report.

(ii).Gross Turnovers:

The firm which have higher turnover will have more complex business activities. Having higher gross turnover , the firm would have technology advancement,large market share, large and complex marketing network, large capital as well as short term investments. Therefore, it is expected to disclose more information than the low turnover firm.

(iii) Rate of Return:

It is conceived that the the enterprise earning higher rate of return on investment would be proud of disclosing more information. such firm will also looks from the point of view of the investors. Therefore, the firm would improve both quality and quantity of information in its annual report. On the other hand, the firm earning low rate of return would not like to provide detailed information about the activities which have caused inefficiency and consequently it leads to less information disclosure in corporate report.

(iv) Size of Enterprise:

The size of enterprise in terms of size of capital employed may influence the quantity of information in a corporate report.. It is perceived that the large sized firm would have complex business activities, complex service, large quantum of production through multiprocessing unit, multiproduct, large capital employment, large size current and fixed assets, Complex management planning and controlling system, improved accounting and reporting system with mechanised systems, business experts and sufficient manpower. Therefore, it is expected that such firm would disclose more information.

EXHIBIT No. 2.4

Disclosure Position of Individual Items

Disclosure percentage	Directors report		Accounting information		Voluntary information		Aggregate (annual report)	
	No. of items	%	No. of items	%	No. of items	%	No. of items	%
00-10	3	5.66	4	2.92	4	16.00	11	5
10-20	5	11.32	2	1.46	7	28.00	15	6
20-30	0	0	4	2.92	3	12.00	7	3
30-40	4	7.55	6	4.38	3	12.00	13	6
40-50	3	5.66	5	3.65	0	0	8	3
50-60	0	0	4	2.92	3	12.00	7	3
60-70	5	9.44	6	4.92	1	4.00	12	5
70-80	9	16.98	9	6.57	1	4.00	19	8
90-100	9	26.47	76	55.47	2	8.00	92	42
Total	53	100.00	137	100.00	25	100.00	215	100

Source : Computed from the figures shown in the annual reports of selected MPSLPEs.

(v) Employment:

An attempt has also been made to find the impact on quantity of information disclosure. Here, it is perceived that the enterprise having more number of employees would be in a position to disclose more information. This is because the firm has sufficient manpower with expertise in accounting and reporting.It is also assumed that the employees would demand more information for bonus, subsidies, facilities, etc.

The conceptual relationship among these company attributes and quantity of information is as below:

Qt=(T,R,C,E,A)

Qt, denotes quantity of information disclosed in Directors report, Accounting information, voluntary and aggregate (Annual Report). T,R,C E,A, stand for gross turnover, rate of return, capital employed, employment and age of enterprise respectively.

While examining the relationship, quantity of information has been assumed as dependent variable and other variables as independent. Further, while examining the relationship of each variables with quality of disclosures, it is assumed that other variables would remain constant.

The relationship of the variables with the quantity of disclosures have been examined by using the "Karle Pearsons Co-efficiant of correlation formula". The 't' test has been used to determine the significance of Co-efficiant of correlation. The calculated 't' value has been compared with table value at 5% and 1% significance level at (n-2) degrees of freedom.

2.4.1 Quantity of Disclosure and Company Characterestics (Corporate Report) :

The relationship of company attributes: Gross turnover, rate of return, capital employed, size of employment and age of enterprise; with the quantity of disclosure have been examined by formulating and testing five null (H_o^1 to H_o^5) hypothesis. The summary results of the five hypothesis (H_o^1 to H_o^5) have been shown in exhibit No. 2.5.

EXHIBIT No 2.5

Summary Results of Relationship between Company Characteristics and Disclosures in Annual Report.

Particulars:	Turnover	Rate of Return	Capital Employed	Employment	Age
Coefficient of correlation (r)	0.4190	-0.0984	0.2371	0.3941	0.6235
Value of "t"	1.7269	0.2966	0.8847	1.2864	2.9840
Degress of freedom (N-2)	14	9	13	9	14
Table value of "t"					
At 5% Significant level	2.145	2.262	2.160	2.262	2.145
At1% Significant level	2.977	3.250	3.012	3.250	2.977
Null of Hypothesis	H^1_0	H^2_0	H^3_0	H^4_0	H^5_0
Result (H_0)	Accepted	Accepted	Accepted	Accepted	Rejected
Degree of correlation observed	high	low	low	high	very high

Source : Computed from the figures shown in annual reports of selectd MPSLPEs.

(i) Gross Turnover and Quantity of Disclosure

In this section, an attempt has been made to find out the relationship between gross turnover and the quantity of disclosures. The following null hypothesis has been formulated and tested.

H^1_o : Gross turnover of the enterprise does not affect the quantity of disclosures.

It is found that the calculated value of "t" is 1.725 < 2.145 and 2.977 at 5% and 1% level of significance for (n-2)=14 degrees of freedom. The aggregate value of 'r' at 0.419 shows that there is positive and high degree of relation between gross turnover and quantity of disclosure. However, the calculated value of 't' is less than the tabulated values both at 5% and 1% levels of significance. Hence, the null hypothesis is accepted. Thus, it shows that though there is relationship of some extent between these two variable but they are not significantly related to each other. Therefore, the gross turnover does not have significant affect on quantity of disclosure in annual reports of a corporate body.

(ii). Rate of Return and Quantity of Disclosure :

In this subsection, the association of rate of return and quantity of disclosure has been tested with the help of the following null hypothesis:

H^2_o : Rate of return on investment and quantity of disclosures are not related to each other.

The exhibit shows that the computed value of 't' is 0.297<2.262 and 3.250 at 5% and 1% sugnificant level at (11-2)=9 degrees of freedom. The value of correlation 'r' - 0.098 shows low and negative relationship between rate of return and quantity of disclosure. The computed value of 't' is less than table values at both 5% and 1% level of significance. Thus, the null hypothesis is accepted. Therefore, it is found that rate of return does not have significant relationship with quantity of disclosures in annual report.

(iii) Size of Enterprise and Quantity of Disclosure.

Here an attempt has been made to find the relationship between the size of enterprise in terms of size of capital employed and quantity of information disclosure. The following null hypothesis has been tested in this regard :

H^3_o : Size of enterprise in terms of size of capital employed does not influence the quantity of information disclosure in annual report.

The exhibit shows that the value of 'r' is 0.257. It indicates low degree of positive relationship between the variables. The calculated value of 't' is 0.885. It is less than the table values of 2.160 and 3.012 at 5% and 1% level of significance respectively at (n-2)=13 degrees of freedom. Thus, the null hypothesis is accepted. It shows that size of enterprise in terms of capital employed does not have significant impact on quantity of information disclosed in annual reports.

(iv) Employment and Quantity of Disclosures:

Here the employment in terms of number of employees in an organisation and its impact on quantity of disclosure has been examined by the following null hypothesis:

H^4_o : Number of employees in an organisation does not influence the quantity of information disclosure in annual report.

The exhibit No. 2.5 shows that the calculated value of 't' is 1.287. It is less than the table value of 't' at 2.262 and 3.250 at 5% and 1% significance levels respectively at (n-2)=9 degrees of freedom. The value of 'r' 0.394 shows positive relationship. The table values of 't' are more than calculated value at both 5% and 1% level of significance. Thus, the null hypothesis is accepted. Therefore, it is found that size of employment does not have significant impact on quantity of disclosure.

(v) Age of Enterprise and Quantity of Disclosure:

The impact of age of enterprise on quantity of disclosure in annual report has been examined by the following null hypothesis:

H^5_o : The older SLPEs do not disclose more information than the new SLPEs in their annual reports.

The results in the exhibit shows that the tabulated values of 't' are 2.145 and 2.977 at 5% and 1% level of significance at (n-2)=14 degrees of freedom. They are less than computed value of 't' at 2.984. The value of 'r' 0.624 is positive and very high. Hence, the null hypothesis is rejected. Therefore, it shows that age of enterprise and quantity of disclosure have positive and significant relationship. It indicates that older SLPEs disclose more information than the newer SLPEs.

2.4.2 Company Characteristics and Quantity of Disclosure in Directors, report.

In this section, an attempt has been made to examine the impact and relationship of company characteristics with the quantity of information disclosures. The null hypotheses numbered from H_o^6 to H_o^{10} were formulated and tested. The results obtained have been shown in exhibit No. 2.6.

(i) Gross Turnover and Quantity of Disclosures:

The association of gross turnover and quantity of disclosure in Directors report has been tested by the following null hypothesis:

H_o^6: Gross turnover and quantity of disclosure in Directors' report are not associated with each other.

The exhibit shows that the co-efficient of correlation 'r' is 0.545. It shows high degree of positive relationship between gross turnover and quantity of disclosure in Directors' report. The calculated value of 't' 2.435 is less than the tabulated values of 't' at 2.145 and 2.977 at 5% and 1% levels of significance at (n-2)=14 degrees of freedom. The calculated value of 't' is more than tabulated value at 5% levels of significance. Hence, the null hypothesis is rejected. Thus, gross turnover and quantity of information in Directors' report have significant relationship with each other. The higher turnover company disclose more information in directors' report.

EXHIBIT No. 2.6

Summary results of Relationship between Quantity of Disclosure in Directors' report and Company Characteristics.

	Company Charecteristics				
Particulars:	**Turnover**	**Rate of Return**	**Capital Employed**	**Employment**	**Age**
Coefficient of correlation (r)	0.5446	-0.3332	0.5054	0.2335	0.1171
Value of "t"	2.4347	0.8536	2.1120	0.7204	0.4412
Degree of freedom (N-2)	14	9	13	9	14
Table value of "t"					
At 5% Significant level	2.145	2.262	2.1600	2.262	2.145
At 1% Significant level	2.977	3.250	3.012	3.250	2.997
Null Hypothese:	H^6_0	H^7_0	H^8_0	H^9_0	H^{10}_0
Result of (H_0)	Rejected	Accepted	Accepted	Accepted	Accepted

Source : Computed from the figures shown in annual reports of the selected MPSLPEs.

(ii) Rate of Return and Quantity of Disclosure in Directors' Report:

The rate of return on capital employed and its relationship with quantity of disclosures have been examined through the formulation and testing of the following null hypothesis:

H_0^7 : Rate of return on capital employed and quantity of disclosures are not related to each other.

The calculated value of 't' is 0.854<2.262 and 3.250 at 5% and 1% level of significance at (n-2)=9 degrees of freedom. The value of 'r' -0.333 shows negative relationship between two variables. The tabulated values of 't' are more than the calculated value both at 5% and 1% levels of significance. Hence, the null hypothesis is accepted. Thus, it is found that rate of return does not have significant effect on quantity of information disclosure in Directors' report.

(iii) Size of Enterprise in terms of Capital employed and Quantity of Disclosure in Directors' Report:

Size of an enterprise in terms of Size of capital employed and its relationship with quantity of disclosure in Directors' Reports have been tested with the help of following null hypothesis :

H_o^8: Size of Capital employed in an organisation does not influence the quantity of disclosure in Directors' Report.

The value of 'r' at 0.505 shows high degree of positive relationship between capital employed and quantity of information disclosure. The calculated value of 't' is 2.112< 2.160 and 3.612 at 5% and 1% levels of significance at (n-2)=13 degrees of freedom. The value calculated is slightly less than the tabulated value of 't' at 5% level of significance. Thus, the null hypothesis is accepted. Therefore, though relationship is at high degree and positive but not found significant. Thus the size of capital employed does not have significant influence on the quantity of disclosures in Directors' Report.

(iv) Size of Employment and quantity of Disclosure in Directors' Report:

Here an attempt has been made to find the relationship between the size of employment and quantity of information disclosed in Directors' Report. The following null hypothesis has been formulated and tested:

H_o^9 : Employment in terms of number of employees in an enterprise does not influence the quantity of information disclosure in Directors' Report.

It is observed from the exhibit that the value of 'r' 0.234 indicates the low degree of positive relationship between size of employment and quantity of disclosure in Directors' Report. The calculated value of 't' is 0.721 which is less than the tabular values of 2.262 and 3.250 at 5% and 1% levels of significance at (n-2)=9 degrees of freedom. Hence, the null hypothesis is accepted. It demostrates that the size of employment in an organisation does not have significant relationship with quantity of information disclosure in Directors' Report.

(V) Age of Enterprise and Quantity of Disclosure in Directors' Report:

The age of an enterprise may have significant association with quantity of disclosure in Directors' Report. The association between age and quantity of information disclosed in Directors' Report have been tested by the following null hypothesis:

H_o^{10}: The age of an enterprise does not affect the quantity of information disclosure in Directors' Reports.

As shown in the exhibit, the value of 'r' at 0.117 shows positive and low degree of relationship persists between age and quantity of disclosure in Directors' report. The calculated value of 't' (0.441) is less than both the tabular values at 2.145 and 2.977 at 5% and 1% levels of significance at (n-2)=14 degrees of freedom. Hence, the null hypothesis is accepted. It reflects that the both variables have very low relationship. The age of enteprise does not have significant influence on quantity of information in Directors' report.

2.4.3 Quantity of Accounting Information Disclosure and Company Characteristics:

It is persumed that the quantity of accounting information disclosure in annual report may be affected by a number of company attributes. In this section, an attempt has been made to examine the relationship between quantity of accounting information and each of the characteristics. They are turnover, rate of return, capital employed, employment and age. The five hypothesis were tested in this regard. The summery results obtained are shown in exhibit No. 2.7.

(i). Gross Turnover and Quantity of Accounting Information:

With a view to examine the relationship between gross turnover and quantity of accounting information disclosed in annual reports, the following null hypothesis was formulated and tested :

H_o^{11}: **Gross turnover of an enterprise does not influence the quantity of statutory accounting information disclosure in annual report.**

It is observed from exhibit that the value of 'r' (0.427) shows positive and high degree of relationship between the gross turnover and quantity of accounting information disclosure. The calculated value of 't' (1.765) is less than both the tabular values of 2.145 and 2.799 at 5% and 1% levels of significance at (n-2)=14 degrees of freedom. Hence, the null hypothesis is accepted. Thus, it is found that turnover does not effect the quantitiy of accounting information disclosure in annual report.

EXHIBIT No. 2.7

Summary Results of Relationship between Quantity of Accounting Information and Company Characterestics.

	Company Charecteristics				
Particulars:	**Turnover**	**Rate of Return**	**Capital Employed**	**Employment**	**Age**
Coefficient of correlation (r)	0.4267	-0.1834	0.3248	0.4344	0.5788
Value of "t"	1.7653	0.5597	1.2382	1.4468	2.6558
Degree of freedom (N-2)	14	9	13	9	14
Table value of "t";					
At 5% Significant level	2.145	2.262	2.160	2.262	2.145
At 1% Significant level 2.997	2.977	3.250	3.612	3.250	3.250
Null Hypothesis	H^{11}_0	H^{12}_0	H^{13}_0	H^{14}_0	H^{15}_0
Results (H_0)	Accepted	Accepted	Accepted	Accepted	Rejected

Source: Computed from the figures shown in annual reports of the selected MPSLPEs.

(ii). Rate of Return and Quantity of Accounting Information:

The following null hypothesis is formulated and tested for examining the relationship between the rate of return and quantity of accounting information disclosure.

H_o^{12} : Rate of return and quantity of statutory accounting information disclosure have no association.

From the exhibit, it is found that the value of 'r' 0.183 shows negative and low degree of relationship between the two variables. The computed value of 't' at 0.560 is less than tabular values at both 2.262 and 3.250 at 5% and 1% levels of significance at (n-2)-9 degrees of freedom. Hence, the null hypothesis is accepted. Thus, it is found that the rate of return does not have influence on quantity of statutory accounting information disclosures.

(iii) Capital Employed and Quantity of Accounting Information:

Size of employed in an enterprise may have influence on the quantity of accounting information disclosure. With a view to find the relationship between these two variables, the following null hypothesis was tested:

H_o^{13} : Capital employed in an enterprise does not affect the quantity of Statutory Accounting Information Disclosure.

The exhibit shows that the computed value of 't' is 1.447. It is less than the tabulated values of 2.160 and 3.612 at 5% and 1% level of significance at (n-2)=13 degrees of freedom. The value of 'r' at 0.325 shows fair degree of positive relationship in both variables. As the calculated value of 't' is less than the tabulated value at both 5% and 1% levels of significance, the null hypothesis is accepted. This demostrates that the size of capital employed in an enterprise does not influence the quantity of statutory accounting information significantly.

(iv) Size of Employment and Quantity of Accounting Information Disclosures

It is intended to examine the association between the size of employment in terms of number of employees in an enteprise and quantity of accounting information disclosure in annual reports. The relationship between these two variables has been tested by following null hypothesis:

H_o^{14}: Size of employment and quantity of statutory accounting information disclosure are not related to each other.

It is observed from the exhibit that the value of Co-efficient of correlation 'r' at 0.434 indicates that the two variables are fairly related to each other positively. The computed value of 't' at 1.447 is less than tabular values of 2.262 and 3.250 at 5% and 1% levels of significance at (n-2)=9 degrees of freedom. Therefore, the null hypothesis is accepted. Thus it is found that the size of employment in terms of number of employees does not have significent influence on quantity of statutory accounting information disclosure in corporate annual report of MPSLPEs.

(v) Age of Enterprise and Quantity of Accounting Information Disclosure.

In this sub section, the association between age of enterprise and quantity of statutory accounting information disclosure have been examined by testing the following null hypothesis:

H_o^{15} : Age of enterprise does not influence the the quantity of disclosures of accounting information in corporate annual report.

It is found from the exhibit that the value of 'r' at0.579 shows high degree of relationship between age of an enterprise and quantity of accounting information disclosure. The calculated value of 't' at 2.659 is higher than 2.145 at 5% levels of significance but less than 2.997 at 1% level significance at (n-2)=14 degrees of freedom. Hence, the null hypothesis is rejected. Thus, it demonstrates that the age of enterprise has significant relationship with quantity of accounting information. The aged enterprise disclose more quantity of accounting information than the new enterprises.

2.3.8 Company Characteristics and Quantity of Voluntary Disclosure in Annual Report.

In this section, an attempt has been made to find out if any significant relationship betweeen each company characteristic and quantity of voluntary disclosures. In order to examine such relationship, five null hypothesis (H_o^{16} to H_o^{20}) were formulated and tested. The summary results of these tests have been shown in exhibit No.2.8

EXHIBIT No. 2.8

Summary Results of Relationship between Quantity of Voluntary Information and Company Characteristics.

	Company Characteristics				
Particulars:	**Turnover**	**Rate of Return**	**Capital Employed**	**Employment**	**Age**
Coefficient of correlation (r)	0.4729	0.1208	0.686	0.2456	0.6533
value of "t"	2.0080	0.3651	0.2479	0.7600	3.2287
Degree of freedom (N-2)	14	9	13	9	14
Table value of "t":					
At 5% Significant level	2.145	2.262	2.160	2.262	2.145
At 1% Significant level	2.977	3.250	3.012	3.250	2.997
Null Hypothesis:	H^{16}_0	H^{17}_0	H^{18}_0	H^{19}_0	H^{20}_0
Results (H_0)	Accepted	Accepted	Accepted	Accepted	Rejected

Source: Computed from the figures shown in annual reports of selected MPSLPEs.

(i) Gross turnover and Quantity of Voluntary Disclosures:

The influence of gross turnover on quantity of voluntary information in annual reports has been examined by following null hypothesis.

H_0^{16}: Gross turnover and quantity of voluntary disclosure in annual reports have no association with each other.

It is found from the exhibit that the value of 'r' 0.473 indicates that there is high degree of positive relationship between two variables. The computed value of 't' at 2.00 is less than tabular values of 2.145 and 2.977 at 5% and 1% levels of significance at (n-2)=14 degrees of freedom. Hence, the null hypothesis is accepted. Thus, it shows that there is high degree of relationship between two variables but the computed value of `t' at 5% level of significance is not found significant. Therefore, it is found that the gross turnover does not effect the quantity of voluntary disclosure in annual reports.

(ii) Rate of Return and Quantity of Voluntary Disclosure.

The influence of rate of return on quantity of voluntary disclosures in annual reports has been examined by following null hypothesis:

H_0^{17}: Rate of return of an enterprise and quantity of voluntary disclosures are not related to each other.

It shows that the calculted value of 't' is 0.365< 2.262 and 3.250 at 5% and 1% levels of significance at (n-2)=9 degrees of freedom. The value of 'r' at 0.121 shows positive relationship between rate of return and quantity of voluntary disclosure. The calculated value of 't' is less than the tabulated values at both 5% and 1% levels of significance. Hence, the null hypothesis is accepted. It shows that there is no significant relationship between rate of return and quantity of voluntary disclosures in annual reports of MPSLPEs.

(iii) Size Of Capital Employed and Quantity of Voluntary Disclosures:

The association of size of capital employed and quantity of voluntary disclosure has been examined by using the following null hypothesis:

H_0^{18}: Size of enterprise in terms of capital employed does not influence the quantity of voluntary disclosure in annual reports.

The value of 'r' at 0.069 shows very low relationship between the size of capital employed and quantity of voluntary disclosure. The calculated value of 't' is 0.248 at (n-2) = 13 degrees of freedom. The tabulated values of 't' at 5% and 1% of significance levels at (n-2)=13 degrees of freedom are 2.160 and 3.012 respectively. The calculated value is less than tabulated values at both 5% and 1% level of significance, Hence, the null hypothesis is accepted. It shows that the size of capital employed does not have significant influence on quantity of voluntary disclosure.

(iv) Size of Employment and Quantity of Voluntary Disclosures:

In this section,an attempt has been to examine the relationship between size of employment in terms of number of employees in an enterprise and quantity of voluntary disclosure in annual reports. The following null hypothesis has been tested:

H_o^{19}: Size of employment in an enterprise does not influence the quantity of voluntary disclosures in annual report.

The exhibit shows that the value of 'r' is 0.247. It indicates positive relationship between size of employment and quantity of voluntary disclosures. The calculated value of 't' is 0.760<2.262 and 3.250 at 5% and 1% levels of significance respectively at (n-2)=9 degrees of freedom. The calculated value is less than tabulated values both at 5% and 1% levels of significance. Therefore, the null hypothesis is accepted. It demonstrates that the size of employment and quantity of voluntary disclosures are not significantly related to each other.

(v) Age of Enterprise and Quantity of Voluntary Disclosures:

Age of enterprise may positively effect on the quantity of voluntary disclosures in annual reports. The relationship between age of enterprise and quantity of voluntary disclosures has been examined by testing the following null hypothesis:

H_o^{20} : Age of the enterprise does not influence the quantity of voluntary disclosures in corporate annual report.

The exhibited results shows that the value of 'r' at 0.653 indicates high degree of positive relationship between age and voluntary disclosure. The calculated value of 't' at 3.229 at (n-2)=14 degrees of freedom is greater than tabulated values of 2.145 and 2.997 at 5% and 1% levels of significance at (n-2)=14 degrees of freedom. Hence, the null hypothesis is rejected. Thus, it is found that age of enterprise has significant influence on quantity of voluntary disclosure. The older enterprise disclose more voluntary information than new enterprises in their corporate annual reports.

REFERENCES

1. Farmer E.R. *Understanding and Interpreting Company Report* Workingham U.K. 1975, p.15.
2. For details, Refer, B. Pradhan, "Corporate Reporting In India :- A Historical Prespactive", *Finance India.* Vol-III.No. IV Dec. 1989-pp. 407-419.
3. For details Refer. K.G.Datta, "Environmental Accounting", *The Management Accountant*, Vol 28. No.10 Oct 1993, p 772-773.
4. David F.Howkings : *Corporate Financial Reporting :- Text and cases*, Richard D. Irwin Inc., Homewood Illonois 1988.p.47
5. Clair Marston *Financial Reporting in India* Croom Helm, London, 1986 p.110.
6. For details Ref. K.L. HANDA,"Financial Information System" in edited book By. J.D.Agrawal, *Accounting for Financial Analysis* Indian Institute of Finance, Delhi 1993 p.416-427.

3

TIMELINESS IN CORPORATE REPORTING

Corporate report carries the information of a corporate entity to its owners, prospective investors, employees, government, research scholers, managers, etc. for their use. The users want the information promptly at the end of accounting period for the prediction of a course of action and decisions. The utility, effectiveness and validity of information in the hands of users depends upon promptness of corporate reporting. The timeliness of corporate report is of a paramont importance and is an important characteristics and objective of corporate reporting[1].

3.1 Timeliness of Corporate Reporting :

Timely disclosure and presentation of information improves the image of the corporate body. It shows managerial efficiency and effectiveness. It reflects quickness in finalisation of accounts and their presentation. It enriches the relationship among management and user groups. It has been pointed out by Bibuti B.Pradhan that "Timeliness of annual reports is an important determinant of their usefulness[2]. Value of the information depends upon a particular person's need or desire to use. However, economic and financial decisions by users of the annual reports are greatly influenced by the time value[3] of information. In general, the value of information diminishes with increase of time lag in publication of the annual report of a concern. Barton Hodge, has presented the value of information in relation to time as follows " The value of information describing the present position has a definate plateau in the range of short lag time. In a general management situation, the same decision would probably be reached whether the information is one minute or one hour old as the lag time extended the value of information began to diminish until a point is finally reached where the value goes to zero"[4]. The need for timeliness in corporate reporting has been recognised by company law, accounting profession, stock exchanges and other relevant acts of incorporation of corporate bodies.

3.1.1 Timeliness in Accounting :

IASC on "frame work for the preparation and presentation of financial statements" states that "if there is undue delay on reporting of information it may loose its relevance. Management may need to balance the relative merits of timely reporting and provision of reliable information. To provide information on timely basis, it may often be necessary to report before all aspects of a transaction or other events are known, thus impairing reliability. Converesly if report is delayed until all aspects are unknown, the information may be highly reliable but of little use to users who have had to make decisions in the interim. In achieving a balance between relevance and reliability, the overriding consideration is how best to satisfy the economic decision making needs of users"[5].

3.1.2 Timeliness in Law :

Legal provisions on timeliness may be grouped as follows :-

(a) General porvisions which are applicable to corporate sector irrespective of their ownership and consideration and

(b) Provisions relating to government companies.

(a) General Provisions :

Section 210 of the companies act 1956 requires the Board of Dirctors to lay the final accounts of the companies before the annual general meeting (AGM) for the period :

(i) in case of the first AGM to the period begining with the incorporation of the company and ending with a day not preceding the meeting day by more than nine months; and

(ii) in case of any subsequent AGM to period begining with the day immediately after the period of the last submitted accounts and ending with a day not preceding the meeting by more than six months.

Under section 166(1)[6] however, a maximum time extension of another 3 months for holding of other than first AGM may be granted for any special season. In case where an extension of time has been granted for holding of AGM, section 210(3)(b) requires that the accounts shall not precede the day of meeting by more than six months and extension so granted. It means final accounts require presentation to shareholders in AGM within 6 months (180 days) of the close of the year, plus a permisible extension of 3 months that means maximum period of 9 months. Section 219 of the companies act 1956, stipulates that final accounts along with auditors' report be sent to every shareholder before 21 days of the date of AGM. This reduces maximum time lag permitted by company law to around 8 months.

(b) Provisions relating to government companies :

Section 619(A) requires the government to prepare an annual report on the working and affairs of a Government company within three months of its AGM. After preparation of the report under reference, as soon as possible this would be laid before both the houses of Parliament in case of the central government companies and legislature in case of the state government company together with a copy of the audit report and the comments there on by the C & AG. Thus, in government company or companies, there is an additional time lag of 3 months over and above the permissible time lag to non government companies. Thus the total time lag in case of the government companies is 12 months or one year.

3.1.3 Literature Review :

In Indian context, studies in recent years on timeliness of corporate reporting are very few. B.B.Pradhan made a study on timeliness, taking a sample of 102 Indian companies. His findings and suggestions are as follows:

1. There has been an improvement in timeliness of announcement of annual report over the period of time, i.e. 1981-85.
2. Net sales and net assets have influenced the delay to some extent.

The findings suggested that the companies should disclose their annual report as early as possible without waiting the statutory time restrictions of Companies Act. 1956.

Sharma R.C.[7] made a study on financial reporting in Central Government Public Enterprises incorporated under Companies Act 1956. His finding on timeliness reporting are:

1. The completeness of audit process will take more time in undertakings which are

(a) Big in size(measured in investment),
(b) Older in age
(c) Audited by a big firm, and
(d) Recording a low rate of return.

2. An undertaking which is audited by a big audit firm is likely to face delay in receiving C & AG comments. The relationships between the time gap in C & AG review and remaining compnay characteristics, i.e. size (Both in terms and investment and turnover) and age of the undertaking were not significant.

3. Size of the undertaking (measured in terms of investment) and age of the undertaking have a significant relationship with its time taken by an undertaking in holding AGM. A big sized undertaking belonging to older age group is likely to hold its AGM late.

4. There was no significant relationship between time lag in holding AGM and remaining two company characteristics i.e. size in terms of gross turnover and the size of audit firm.

5. The earning record of an enterprise does not necessarily help in early receipt of C & AG review and timely holding of AGM.

The relevant literature reviewed shows that no study has so for been conducted with an aim to evaluate timeliness of corporate reporting in SLPEs in India.

3.1.4 Present study :

The study aims :

(i) to ascertain various type of time lags

(ii) to analysis the extent and variations in timeliness of corporate reporting.

(iii) to examine relationship between corporate characteristics, viz. size, age, rate of return, etc. and timelness in corporate reporting.

An attempt has been made to identify total time lag of information disclosure for each enterprise and then an aggregate position of the sample. The contributary factors to total time lag have also been identified. They includes auditor's time lag, comptroller and auditor general's time lag and reporting time lag. The time lag have been worked out on the basis of dates of signatories in annual reports, date of last day of accounting year and date of annual general meeting. The different time lags have been identified and computed as follows :

(i) Total time lag :

The total time lag of corporate reporting is identified as difference between the last day of the accounting year and the day of annual general meeting for finalization and display of final accounts. This lag has been computed as follows :

Date of annual general meeting	- - -
Less-Date of last day of accounting year	- - -
Total time lag	- - -

(ii) Auditor time lag :

The auditors time lag is the difference between the date of auditors signature and the date of last day of accounting year. It has been arrived as follows :

Date of auditors signature on audit report	- - -
Less-Date of last day of accounting year	- - -
Auditors time lag	- - -

(iii) C & AG's time lag :

The C & AG's time lag has been taken as the difference between Date of C & AG's signature on C & AG's report and the date of auditors signature on audited report

This has been computed as follows :

Date of C & AG's signature	- - -
Less-Date of auditors signature on audit report	- - -
C & AG's time lag	- - -

(iv) Reporting time lag :

The reporting lag is the time lag which is equal to the difference between the date of annual general meeting and date of signature of C & AGs on C & AG's report. In some cases where annual reports did not contain the A & AG's report. In such cases reporting lag has been considered as the difference between date of annual general meeting and date of auditors' report. The reporting time lag has been computed as follows :

Date of AGM	- - -
Less-Date of C & AG's signature	- - -
Reporting time lag	- - -

3.2 Extent and Variations in Timeliness :

For each MPSLPE, the time lag was identified and computed. Then the analysis was made for the evaluation of timeliness of MPSLPEs. The average time lag for each type of time lag have been computed. Then, the averages were further analysed to understand the range and variations in the sample among the enterprises. The statistical tools used for this purpose are Arthimatic mean, Range, Standard deviation and Co-efficient of variation.

3.2.1. Timeliness position of individual MPSLPE :

Exhibit No. 3.1 given on next page shows the timeliness position of each MPSLPE and their average. The timeliness position of individual MPSLPE in respect of Audit time lag, C & AG's time lag, reporting time lag and total time lag is analysed below :

(i) The exhibit shows that audit time lag of individual SLPE varies between 60 and 2291 days. Average audit time lag is 1030.13 days. On the basis of audited time lag, the following grouping has been made :

Audit time lag (days)	No. of MPSLPES	Percentage Share in Total
0-100	1	6.25
100-500	2	12.50
500-1000	8	00.00
1000-2000	4	25.00
2000-2500	1	6.25
	16	100.00

This shows that half of the PEs has the audit time lag in between 500 and 1000 days. Further time lag of 25% PEs varies between 1500 and 2000 days. It clearly shows that the delay in corporate reporting is mainly due to delay in finalisation of accounts and its subsequent audit.

EXHIBIT No. 3.1

Statement of Time Lag of Individual MPSLPEs

Name of MPSLPEs	Time lag (Day) Audit lag	C&AGs lag	Reporting lag	Total lag
1. Agro Industries Development Corporation	1589	70	46	1705
2. Forest Development Corporation	2291	-	229	2520
3. Small Industries Development Corporation	989	82	48	1119
4. Urja Vikas Nigam	791	224	80	1095
5. Finance Corporation	60	-	28	88
6. Police Housing	792	11	50	853

	Corporation				
7.	Seeds and Farm Development Corporation	774	-	45	819
8.	Industrial Development Corporation	1706	-	233	1939
9.	State Industries Corporation	1687	-	151	1838
10.	State Road Transport	734	-	45	779
11.	Electronic Development Corporation	641	56	22	719
12.	Land Development Corporation	252	-	295	547
13.	Textile Corporation	1944	69	25	2038
14.	Setu Nirman Nigam	503	60	30	593
15.	Nagarik Apurti Nigam	481	66	97	644
16.	Electricity Board	902	-	40	942
	Average for all SLPEs.	1030.13	79.75	95.60	1139.88

Source: Complied and Computed from Annual Reports of the MPSLPEs.

(ii) It is also found that 8 annual reports out of 16 contains comments of C & AG's. The following is the classified position:

C&AG's time lag	No. of MPSLPEs	Percentage Share in Total
0-50	1	12.5
50-100	6	75
100-224	1	12.5
	8	100.00

This time lag varies between 11 and 224 days. It is found that 87.5% of the MPSLPEs get their accounts and audit report reviewed within 100 days. However, 75% of PEs take 50 to 100 days time. The average C & AG's time lag is 79.75 days. It is much less than audit time lag.

(iii) The time taken by MPSLPEs in holding their annual general meeting of after the completion of audit and C & AGs review varies between 22 and 295 days. The average reporting time lag is 95.60 days. The following is the position :

Reporting time lag	No. of MPSLPEs	Percentage Share of Total
0-50	10	62.5
50-100	2	12.5

100-150	0	0
150-200	1	6.75
200-250	2	12.50
250-300	1	6.75
	16	100.00

The grouping clearly shows that the majority of the MPSLPEs take upto 50 days time in holding the annual general meeting after completion of audit and review of C & AGs lag. However, greater variation is found in groups,

(iv) Total time taken in holding annual general meeting from the date of last day of accunting year varies between 88 and 2520 days. The average is 1139.88 days. The following grouping shows timeliness of corporate reporting position of individual MPSLPEs

Total time lag	No. of MPSLPEs	Percentage Share in Total
0-100	1	6.25
100-500	0	0
500-1000	8	50.00
1000-1500	2	12.50
1500-2000	3	18.75
2000-2520	2	12.50
	16	100.00

The above classification shows that 43.25% half of the MPSLPEs take more than 1000 day to hold the annual general meeting. There are only 8 companies which take 500 to 1000 days in holding annual general meeting.

3.2.2 Variations of Timeliness Position in MPSLPEs :

Exhibit No. 3.2 shows the range and coefficient of range of timeliness position of MPSLPEs

EXHIBIT No. 3.2

Variation of Timeliness in Selected MPSLPEs

Type of time lag	Range (days)	Coefficient of range	Mean(x) (days)	0	C.V. %	Order of Variation , Uniformity
Audit lag	2291-60=2231	0.9489	1030	635.10	61.55	III II

C&AGs lag	224-11=213	0.9064	79.75	57.98	72.49	II	III
Reporting lag	295-22=273	0.8612	95.60	85.53	89.47	II	IV
Total lag	2520-88=2432	0.9325	1139.88	646.73	56.74	IV	I

Source : Compiled and computed from the information contained in annual reports of individual units.

From the figures calculated above, following broad generalisations may be derived :

(i) When we look at the variations, we find that the range of the audit lag is the highest. It has constituted 92% of the total lag. On the other hand, the C & AGs reporting lag has an insignificant share varying between 3% and 5%.

(ii) The co-efficient of range has not varied much. It clearly indicates that the variations in individual MPSLPEs are insignificant.

(iii) When we look at the variations in terms of coefficient of variation, We find that the variation in case of reporting and C & AG. time lags are wide and significant. The audit lag variations are almost uniform in case of all the MPSLPEs. However, we may conclude that the audit lag of all the MPSLPEs needs immediate attention.

3.2.4. Timeliness and Statutory Period :

The following hypothesis was formulated and tested for evaluating relationship between average timeliness of MPSLPEs with statutory period:

H_o : MPSLPEs on an average release their annual reports within the maximum period allowed by law (9 months or 270 days)

(In this hypothesis, the release of annual report is assumed to be on the day of AGM)

The hypothesis is tested by using the 't' test. The formula of "t" test is as follows :

$$t = \frac{(X - Y) \times (N)^{1/2}}{S}$$

$$t = \frac{(1139.82 - 270) \times (16)^{1/2}}{646.73}$$

$$t = \frac{3479.52}{646.73} = 5.38$$

The table value of 't' at 16 degrees of freedom and at 5% significance level is 1.746 which is less than the computed value. Hence, the null hypothesis is rejected. That indicates that the MPSLPEs on an average do not release their annual reports within 270 days from the date of last day of accounting year. In other words, MPSLPEs do not hold their annual general meeting within the period allowed by law.

3.2.4 Timeliness in Different Forms of MPSLPEs.

An attempt has been made to ascertain the timeliness position in different forms of MPSLPEs. The total time lag against each type of form has been shown in Exhibit No. 3.3.

EXHIBIT No. 3.3
Form of the Enterprise and the Time Lag

Form of the MPSLPEs	Time lag (year) Less than 9 months	1-2	2-3	3-4	4-5	5-6	6-7	Total Company
1. Company form (Registered Under Indian Companies Act. 1956	-	3	1	2	1	3	1	11
2. Statutory form (established under special act of legislature)	1	1	1	-	-	-	-	3
3. Societies form (Registered under societies REgistration Act.)	-	-	1	-	1	-	-	2
Total	1	4	2	2	2	3	1	16

Source : Computed from the figures shown in exhibit No. 3.1

The Exhibit No. 3.3 shows that the company form of MPSLPEs takes more time to release their annual report than statutory and societies form of enterprises. Statutory form of MPSLPEs are disclosing the information earlier than other two forms. Only one MPSLPE is statutory which has disclosed the information within stipulated legal time period of nine months.

3.3 Timeliness and Company Characteristics

It is perceived that some corporate attributes may have influence on timeliness of corporate reporting. An attempt has been made to find out the extent of relationship of following corporate attributes with timeliness.

(i) Age :

It is assumed that as the firm grows older as its experience and expertise would increase. Therefore, the accounting would be smooth and it would result timely finalisation of accounts, auditing and C & AG's review. Viewed from different angle, the older firms would have to deal with accounting problems relating to earlier periods. With an increase in age and size, accounting would become more complex and hence delay in compilation of accounts, audit and C & AGs' review.

(ii) Turnover :

It is expected that an enterprise having larger turnover would have complex problems of multiproduct sales, large marketing and distribution net work, heavy spending on advertisments etc. It would lead to delay in finalisation of accounts, completion of audit and conduct of review by C & AGs'.

(iii) Capital Employed :

It is expected that big enterprises in terms of capital employed, possessing large financial and physical resources, would be in a position to have expert staff and mechanical accounting system. Therefore, it is expected smooth accounting and early finalisation of accounts and other matters. Viewed from different angle, big enterprise would have complex activities, various products and big plants. For this structure, they have to maintain complex accounting structure. This may lead to delay in finalisation of accounts and other matters.

(iv) Rate of Turnover :

It is expected that the enterprise which achieve higher rate of turnover to the satisfaction of management of an enterprise would record its transaction at the earliest possible. Hence firm which have higher rate of turnover would finalise its account audit and C & AGs review at an early date. The reporting mechanism of the firm would also take less time than low turnover firms.

(v) Employment :

It is expected that an enterprise having larger manpower in terms of number of personnel employed in an enterprise would execute the activities timely. This would lead to early finalisation of accounts, audit and review by C & AG. Viewed from different angle, more employees may not create productive work culture in the enterprise.

(vi) Rate of return :

It is said that an enterprise earning higher rate of return would like to put its achievement on record at earliest possible movement, and therefore, such enterprise expediate the finalisation of accounts and other matters. It would also like to conduct Annual general meeting at earliest date. On the other hand, the enterprise which is earning below expectation may defer announcement and may not be interested in early compilation of accounts, audit and C & AG's review.

To test the validity of relationship of each company characteristics with timeliness, the following conceptual relationship is assumed:

TL = f (A, T, Ce, Rt, E, Rr)

TL denotes total time lag i.e. aggregate of Audit lag, C & AGs lag and reporting lag.

A, T, Ce, Rt, E, and Rr denotes Age, Turnover, Capital Employed, Rate of turnover, Employment and Rate of return respectively. While examining reletionship of each variable with time lags, time lag is assumed as independent variable. The relationship of variables have been examined by formulating various hypothesis. Karl Pearson Co-efficient of correlation formula and the 't' test were used to find out the extent of relationship and the significance of co-efficient of correlation. The calculated value of 't' has been compared with table values at 5% and 1% significant level at (N-2) degrees of freedom.

3.4.1 Total Time Lag and Company Characteristics :

To find out the relationship between total time lag and each company chracteristics, various hypothesis were formulated and tested. The summary results are shown in exhibit No. 3.4

(i) Age and Total Time Lag :

An attempt has been made to find out the existing relationship between age of enterprise and timeliness (total time lag of corporate reporting). The following is null hypothesis :

H_o^{21} : Age of the enterprise does not influence the timeliness of corporate reporting.

Exhibit 3.4 shows that calculated 't' value is 0.325 < 2.145 and 2.977 at 5% and 1% level of significance respectively for (N-2) = 14 degree of freedom. The value of 'r' (-0.081) shows negative relationship between age and timeliness. The tabulated values of 't' is greater than calculated value at 5% and 1% level of significance. Hence, the null hypothesis is accepted. Thus it appears that there is no significant association between age and timeliness (total time lag).

(ii) Turnover and Timeliness :

The relationship between turnover and timeliness has been tested by formulating and testing the follwing null hypothesis :

H_o^{22} : Gross turnover has no relationship with timeliness of information disclosure.

As various parameters shown in exhibit No. 3.4., the calculated value of 't'is 0.578 < 2.168 and 3.012 at 5% and 1% level of significance respectively for (N-2) = 13 degrees of freedom. The value of (r) -0.158 shows negative relationship between turnover and timeliness. The calculated value of 't' is less than table values of 't' at both 5% and 1% significance level. Hence, the null hypothesis is accepted. It shows that there is no significant relationship between gross turnover and timeliness.

EXHIBIT No. 3.4

Total Time Lag and Company Characteristics

	:			Company Characteristics		
Particulars	**: Age**	**Turn over**	**Capital Employed**	**Rate of Turnover**	**Employment**	**Rate of Return**
Coefficient of correlation (r)	-0.081	-0.158	-0.124	-0.188	-0.159	-0.304
Value of "t"	0.325	0.578	0.194	0.455	0.956	
Degrees of free-dom (N-2)	14	13	13	13	8	9
Table value of "t"						
at 5% Significant level	2.145	2.160	2.160	2.160	2.306	2.262
at 1% Significant	2.977	3.012	3.012	3.012	3.355	3.250
Hypothesis (H_0)	H^{21}_0	H^{22}_0	H^{23}_0	H^{24}_0	H^{25}_0	H^{26}_0
Result of Null hypothesis	A	A	A	A	A	A
Degree of correlation	L	L	L	L	L	L

Source : Computed from information shown in the annual reports of selected MPSLPEs.

(iii) Capital Employed and Timeliness :

Relationship between capital employed and total time lag has been tested by formulating and testing the following null hypothesis:

H_o^{23} : Size of an enterprise in terms of capital employed and timeliness of corporate reporting are not related to each other.

Exhibit No. 3.4 shows that the calculated value of 't' 0.452 is less than table values of 2.168 and 3.012 at 5% and 1% level significant level of(N-2)= 13 degrees of freedom. The value of 'r' (-0.124) indicates that there is negative relationship between capital employed and total time lag. The table value of 't' is greater than computed value of 't' at 5% and 1% significant level. Hence, the null hypothesis is accepted. Thus it appears that there is no significant relationship between capital employed and total time lag.

(iv). Rate of Turnover and Timeliness :

Relationship between rate of turnover and total time lag has been tested by formulating and testing the following null hypothesis

H_o^{24} : Rate of turnover and timeliness of corporate reporting has no relationship with each other.

Exhibit No. 3.4 shows that the calculated value of 't' is 0.194 < 2.168 and 3.012 at 5% and 1% level of significant at (N-2)=13 degrees of freedom. The value of 'r' (-0.188) shows that there is low and negative relationship. The tabulated values of 't' is higher than the calculated value of 't' at 5% and 1% significant level. Hence, the null hypothesis is accepted. Thus it shows that there is no significant relationship between the rate of turnover and total time lag.

(v). Employment and Timeliness :

The relationship between employees in an enterprise and total time lag has been examined with formulation of and testing the following null hypothesis :

H_o^{25} : Size of employment of an enterprise does not influence the timeliness of corporate reporting.

The exhibit 3.4 shows that the 't' value is 0.453 < 2.308 and 3.356 at 5% and 1% significant level at (N-2) = 8 degrees of freedom. The value of 'r' (-0.153) shows that there is negative relationship between employment and timeliness (total time). The tabulated values of 't' are higher than calculated value of t at 5% and 1% significant level. Hence, the null hypothesis is accepted. Thus, it shows, that there is no significant relationship between size of employment and total time lag.

(vi) Rate of Return and Timeliness :

An attempt has also been made to examine the relationship between rate of return and total time lag by formulating and testing the following hypothesis :

H_o^{26} : Rate of return of MPSLPEs does not influence the timeliness of corporate reporting.

The exhibit 3.4 shows that the calculated 't' value is 0.956 < 2.262 and 3.250 at 5% and 1% significant level respectively at (N-2)=9, degrees of freedom. The value of 'r' (-0.304) shows that there is negative relationship between these two variables. The tabulated values of 't' are higher than calculated value at both 5% and 1% level of significance. Hence, the null hypothesis is accepted and the rate of return of MPSLPEs does not influence the total time lag significantly.

3.3.2 Audit Lag and Company Characteristics :

In this section, an attempt has been made to know whether there is any relationship between audit lag and each company characteristics. The null hypotheses formulated and tested in this regard (numbering H^{27}_o to H^{32}_o) and the summary results have been shown in Exhibit No. 3.5.

EXHIBIT No. 3.5

Timeliness of Audit Lag and Company Characteristics

:	Company Characteristics					
Particulars	**: Age**	**Turn over**	**Capital Employed**	**Rate of Turnover**	**Employment**	**Rate of Return**
Coefficient of correlation (r)	-0.153	-0.133	-0.096	-0.95	-0.046	-0.316
Value of "t"	0.581	0.483	0.347	0.344	0.131	0.999
Degree of freedom (N-2)	14	13	13	13	8	9
Table value of "t"						
at 5% Significant level	2.145	2.160	2.160	2.160	2.306	2.262
at 1% Significant level	2.977	3.012	3.012	3.012	3.355	3.250

Hypothesis (H_0)	H^{27}_0	H^{28}_0	H^{29}_0	H^{30}_0	H^{31}_0	H^{32}_0
Result of Null hypothesis	A	A	A	A	A	A
Degree of correlation	V/L	V/L	V/L	V/L	V/L	V/L

Source : Computed from the information given in annual reports of selected MPSLPEs

(i). Age and Audit Lag :

Here an attempt has been made to find the relationship between age and audit lag by formulating and testing the following null hypothesis:

H_o^{27} : Age of an enterprise does not influence the time taken in audit of final accounts.

The exhibit shows that the computed value of 't'is 0.581 < 2.145 and 2.977 at 5% and 1% level of significance and at (N-2)=14 degrees of freedom. The value of 'r' (0.153) indicates low and negative relationship between age and audit lag. The tabulated values of 't' are more than computed value at 5% and 1% level of significance. Hence, the null hypothesis is accepted. Thus, it appears that age of PE and audit lag do not have significant relationship.

(ii) Turnover and Audit Lag :

The association between these two variables has been examined with the following null hypothesis :

H_o^{28} : Turnover in an enterprise does not influence the time taken in audit of the final accounts.

The calculated value of "t" is 0.483<2.168 and 3.012 at 5% and 1% significant level at (n-2)=13 degrees of freedom. The "r" value (-0.133) shows low and negative relationship. The tabulated values of "t" are more than calculated value of "t" at both at 5% and 1% significant level. Hence the null hypothesis is accepted. Therefore, it reflects that there is no significant relationship between turnover and time taken in auditing the accounts of MPSLPEs.

(iii) Capital Employed and Time taken in Audit (Audit Lag)

The relationship between size of MPSLPE in terms of Capital employed and time taken in auditing the accounts have been examined by the following null hypothesis:

H_o^{29} : Size of Capital employed in the MPSLPEs does not have any relationship with Audit lag.

The calculated value of "t" 0.347 is less than 2.168 and 3.012 at 5% and 1% level of significance, at (N-2)=13 degrees of freedom. The value of "r" (-0.096) of shows negative and very low degree of relationship between these variables. The table of values of "t" are more than calculated value of 't' at both 5% and 1% level of significance. Therefore, the null hypothesis is accepted. Thus, it shows that the size of capital employed in MPSLPEs does not have significant relationship with audit time lag.

(iv) Rate of Turnover and Audit Lag :

Influence of rate of turnover on audit time lag has been examined by formulating and testing the following null hypothesis:

H_o^{30}: Rate of turnover does not effect the audit time lag.

The computed value of 't' is 0.344 which is less than table values of 't' at 2.168 and 3.012 at 5% and 1% level of significance at (N-2)=13 degrees of freedom. Hence, the null hypothesis is accepted. The value of 'r' -0.095 shows very low and negative relationship. Therefore, it is found that the rate of turnover does not have significant relationship with time taken in auditing the account of MPSLPEs.

(v) Size of Empolyment and Audit Lag.

Here, an attempt has been made to examine the relationship between size of employment in terms of number of employees and time taken in audit by formulating and testing the following null hypothesis :

H_o^{31}: Size of employment in MPSLPEs does not influence the audit time lag.

From the exhibit No 3.5, it is found that calculated value of 't' is 0.131 < 2.306 and 3.355 at 5% and 1% level of significance respectively at (N-2)=8 degrees of freedom. The tabulated values of 't' are more that calculated value at 5% and 1% level of significance. Therefore, the null hypothesis is accepted. Thus, the size of employment in terms of number of employees does not have significant influence on time lag of audit.

(vi) Rate of Return and Audit Lag :

Influence of rate of return on audit time lag has been examined by formulating and testing the following hypothesis:

H_o^{32} : Rate of return has no influence on Audit Time Lag.

The exhibit No. 3.5 shows that the computed value of 't' is 0.999 < 2.262 and 3.250 at 5% and 1% level of significance at (n-2) = 9 degrees of freedom. The value of 'r' (-0.316) shows negative relationship. The tabulated values of 't' at 5% and 1% level is more than calculated value of 't'. Thus, the null hypothesis is accepted. Therefore, rate of return does not have significant relationship with audit time lag.

3.3.3 C & AG's Time Lag and Company Characteristics:

C & AGs time lag and its relationship with each selected company characteristics has been examined by formulating and testing various null hypotheses. The summary results have been shown in exhibit No. 3.6.

EXHIBIT No. 3.6

C & AGs Time Lag and Company Characteristics

	Company Characteristics					
Particulars	**: Age**	**Turn over**	**Capital Employed**	**Rate of Turnover**	**Employment**	**Rate of Return**
Coefficient of correlation (r)	-0.161	-0.118	-0.300	-0.52	-0.433	0.839
Value of "t"	0.400	0.292	0.772	0.128	0.961	8.502
Degress of freedom (N-2)	6	6	6	6	4	2
Table value of "t"						
at 5% Significant level	2.447	2.447	2.447	2.447	2.776	4.303
at 1% Significant level	3.707	3.707	3.707	3.707	4.604	9.925
Hypothesis (H_0)	H^{33}_0	H^{34}_0	H^{35}_0	H^{36}_0	H^{37}_0	H^{38}_0
Result of Null hypothesis	A	A	A	A	A	A
Degree of correlation	V/L	V/L	V/L	V/L	LOW	V/L

Source : Computed from the information shown in annual reports of selected MPSLPEs

(i) Age of MPSLPEs and C & AG's Time Lag :

In order to examine the relationship between C & AGs time lag and age of enterprise, the following null hypothesis was formulated and tested :

H_o^{33} : Age of MPSLPEs and C & AGs time lag are not associated with each other.

The exhibit No. 3.6 shows that the calculated 't' value is 0.400 < 2.447 and 3.707 at 5% and 1% level of significance respectively at (n-2)=6 degrees of freedom. The 'r' value (-0.101) shows that the two variables are negatively related to each other. The table value of 't' is more than calculated value of 't' both at 5% and 1% level of significance. Hence, the null hypothesis is accepted. Thus, it shows that age of enterprise does not have significant influence on C & AG's time lag.

(ii) Turnover and C & AGs Time Lag :

With a view to examine the relationship between these variables, the following null hypothesis was formulated and tested:

H_o^{34} : Turnover does not influence C & AGs time lag.

From the exhibit No. 3.6, it is found that the calculated value of 't' is 0.292 < 2.447 and 3.707 at 5% and 1% significance level at (n-2)=6, degrees of freedom. The value of'r' (0.118) shows low and negative relationship. The tabulated values of 't' are more than calculated value at 5% and 1% level of significance. Hence, the null hypothesis is accepted. Therefore, it shows that the turnover in MPSLPEs does not have any significant influence on time lag in C & AG's review.

(iii) Capital Employed and Time Lag of C & AG :

The relationship between size of capital employed in MPSLPEs and C & AGs time lag has been examined by of formulating and testing the following null hypothesis :

H_o^{35} : Size of capital employed does not influence the C & AG's time lag.

The exhibit No. 3.6 shows that the calculated value of 't' is 0.772 < 2.447 and 3.707 at 5% and 1% level of significance respectively at (n-2)=6 degrees of freedom. The value of 'r' (-0.161) shows that the variables are related to each other. The value of calculated 't'' is less than both at 5% and 1% significance level. Hence,the null hypothesis is accepted. Thus, it is found that size of capital employed does not influence the C & AG's time lag.

(iv) Rate of Turnover and C & AG's Time Lag :

Here, an attempt has been made to find the relationship between rate of turnover and C & AGs time lag. The following null hypothesis has been formulated and tested :

H_o^{36} : Rate of turnover does not have relationship with C & AG's time lag.

From the exhibit No. 3.6, it is found that the calculated value of 't' is 0.128 which is less than table values at 2.247 and 3.707 at 5% and 1% significance level respectively and (n-2)=6 degrees of freedom. The value of 'r' is (-0.052) which is very low and negative. Thus the null hypothesis is accepted. It is found that the rate of turnover does not have significant relationship with C & AG's time lag.

(v) Size of Employment and C & AGs Time Lag :

In this section, the relationship between size of employment in terms of number of employees in MPSLPEs and C & AGs time lag has been examined by formulating and testing the following null hypothesis:

H_o^{37} : Size of employment does not influence the C & AGs time lag.

The exhibit No.3.6 shows that the calculated 't' value is 0.961 < 2.776 and 4.604 at 5% and 1% significance level respectively at (n-2)=4 degrees of freedom. The value of 'r' - 0.433 shows high degree of negative relationship. The tabulated values of 't' are higher than the computed value of 't' at 5% and 1% level of significance. Hence the null hypothesis is accepted. Therefore, it is found that the size of employment in terms of number of employees does not influence in C & AGs time lag.

(vi) Rate of Return and C & AGs Time Lag :

The relationship between rate of return and C & AGs time lag has been tested by formulating and testing the following hypothesis :

H_o^{38} : Rate of return does not influence C & AGs time lag

The exhibit No. 3.6, shows that the calculated value of 't' is 8.582. It is greater than tabulated values of 4.303 at 5% significance level but less than the 9.925 at 1% significance level at (n-2)=2 degrees of freedom. Hence, the null hypothesis at 5% significance level is rejected. Thus, the rate of return has significant influence on C & AGs time lag.

3.3.4. Relationship between Reporting Time Lag and Company Characteristics :

The relationship between the holding the annual general meeting time lag and the each company characteristics has been examined by formulating and testing various hypotheses. The various summary results revealed in the examination of relationship between those two variables are shown in the exhibit No. 3.7.

EXHIBIT No. 3.7

Reporting Time Lag and Company Characteristics

Particulars	Company Characteristics					
	: Age	Turn over	Capital Employed	Rate of Turnover	Employment	Rate of Return
Coefficient of correlation (r)	-0.009	-0.186	-0.174	0.012	-0.231	-0.333
Value of "t"	0.031	0.651	0.612	0.0425	0.623	1.059
Degree of freedom (N-2)	13	12	12	12	7	9
Table value of "t" at 5% Significant level	2.160	2.179	2.179	2.179	2.365	2.262
at 1% Significant level	3.012	3.055	3.055	3.055	3.499	3.250
Hypothesis (H_0)	H^{39}_0	H^{40}_0	H^{41}_0	H^{42}_0	H^{43}_0	H^{44}_0
Result of Null hypothesis	A	A	A	A	A	A
Degree of correlation	L	L	L	L	L	L

Source : Computed from the information given in annual reports of selected MPSLPEs

(i) Age and Reporting Time Lag.

The relationship between age of enterprise and time taken in holding AGM has been examined by formulating and testing the following null hypothesis:

H_o^{39} : Age of enterprise and reporting time lag are not related to each other.

Exhibit No. 3.7 shows that the calculated 't' value of0.031 is less than table values of 't' at 2.160 and 3.012 at 5% and 1% significance level respectively at (n-2)=13 degrees of freedom. The value of 'r'(-0.089) is very low and negative. Hence, the null hypothesis is accepted. Thus the age of enterprise does not have significant relationship with reporting time lag.

(ii) Turnover and Reporting Time Lag

The relationship between turnover in enterprise and time taken in holding the annual general meeting has been examined by formulating and testing the following null hypothesis :

H_o^{40} : Turnover of enterprise does not influence the time lag of holding annual general meeting.

The results have been shown in exhibit No. 3.7. It is seen that the calculated value of 't' 0.651 is less than 2.179 and 3.055 at 5% and 1% level of significance at (n-2)=12 degrees of freedom. The value for 'r' (-0.186) shows negative relationship between the two variables. The table values of 't' at 5% and 1% level of significance is more than the calculated value of 't'. Hence, the null hypothesis is accepted. Therefore, it is found that turnover in enterprise does not have significant relationship with reporting time lag.

(iii) Capital Employed and Reporting Time Lag :

The relationship between capital employed and reporting time lag has been examined by the formulating and testing the null hypothesis as follows :

H_o^{41} : Size of capital employed does not influence the reporting time lag.

The exhibit 3.7 shows that the calculated value of 't' is 0.612 < 2.179 and 3.055 at 5% and 1% significant level at (n-2)=12 degrees of freedom. The value of 'r' (-0.174) shows negative relationship. The table values of 't' are higher than calculated value of 't' at 5% and 1% significant level. Hence, the null hypothesis is accepted. It is found that size of capital employed does not have significant relationship with reporting time lag.

(iv) Rate of Turnover and Reporting Time Lag :

Here, an attempt has been made to examine the relationship between rate of turnover and reporting time lag by formulating and testing the following null hypothesis:

H_o^{42} : Rate of turnover and reporting lag are not related to each other.

Exhibit 3.7 indicates that the calculated value of 't' 0.043 <2.179 and 3.055 at 5% and 1% level of significance and at (n-2)= 12 degrees of freedeom. The value of "r"(0.012) shows low and positive relationship . The table values of "t" are greater than calculated value of "t" at 5% and 1% level of significance. Hence, null hypothosis is accepted. It is found that rate of turnover does not influence the reporting time lag significantly.

(v) Size of Employment and Reporting Time Lag:

The relationship between size of employment in terms of number of employees in MPSLPEs and reporting time lag has been tested by the following null hypothesis:

H_o^{43} : Size of employment does not influence the reporting time lag.

The exhibit No. 3.7 shows that the value of 'r' shows (-0.231) negative relationship between size of employment and reporting time lag . The calculated value of 't' is 0.623 which is less than tabulated values of 't' 2.365 and 3.499 at 5% and 1% level of significance respectively and at (n-2)=7 degrees of freedom. Therefore, the null hypothesis is accepted. It is found that the size of employment in MPSLPESs does not have significant effect on the time lag of holding annual general meeting.

(vi) Rate of Return and Reporting Time Lag:

The relationship between rate of return on capital employed and reporting time lag has been examined by formulating and testing the following null hypothesis:

H_o^{44}: Rate of return on capital employed does not influence the reporting time lag of an enterprise

It is found from the exhibit No. 3.7 that the calculated 't' value is 1.059 < 2.262 and 3.250 at 5% and 1% level of significance at (n-2)=9 degrees of freedom. The value of 'r' (-0.333) shows that the two variables are negatively related. The tabulated values of 't' is more than calculated value at both 5% and 1% level of significance. Thus, the null hypothesis is accepted. It is found from the above analysis that rate of return on capital employed does not have significant influence on reporting time lag.

REFERENCES

1. B.B.Pradhan, "Corporate Reporting In India : A Historical Perspective" *Finance India*, Vol-III No.IV Dec 1989, p 407-420.

2. B.B.Pradhan, "An Analysis on timeliness of Annual Report" *Finance India*, Vol-III No.1 March 1989; p.35-48.

3. E.J.Mishan, *Cost Benefit Analysis*, Unwin Hyman, Boston, 1984, pp. 305-310.

4. Beartow Hodge, Robert A. Flick, Brain Honess, *Management of Information System*, Irvin Wevell U.K. 1986, p.473.

5. IASC On "Frame work for the Preparation and Presentation of Financial Statement", 1986.

6. Companies Act 1956.

7. Sharma, R.C. *Financial Reporting in Public Enterprises*, Tiwari publications, Delhi, 1991, p.145.

4

READABILITY OF CORPORATE REPORT

The annual reports of public enterprises are meant for public appraisal about the functioning of the enterprise. Therefore, the contents of the reports should be easily readable and understandable by a common person in the public. The management should take into account the reading ability and understanding capacity of readers while writing the report. It should write the report in simple language by using simple and familiar words, short sentences and short paragraphs. In general for effective communication, the readability of annual report should be within reading and understanding level of the users.

4.1 Communication and Readability:

The effectiveness of a written communication largely depends upon the extent to which the receipient can read and understand the message[1]. It also depends upon the writing skill and style of the writer[2]. It can be improved by organisation of the materials in fast moving and orderly form. Such arrangement creates interest and brings satisfaction to readers. The linguistic clarity, visual simplicity and clear statements improve the presentation and quality of contents. The improvement in written presentation helps the reader to grasp more quickly and exactly what the writer wants to communicate the message.The readability as a measuring tool of written presentation helps to measure the reading ability required to read and understand the message. It enables the writer to have an objective evaluation of a report or text and provides the feedback to modify the writings to make them purposive[3]

4.1.1 Readability Measurements :

Robert Gunning[4] developed a formula to measure the difficulty of reading matter by the use of a "yardstick'. He wanted a tool which would be (1) easy to use, (2) reliable in measurement , and (3) valuable to call a writers attention to the factors which cause readers most difficulty. After much experimentation, he built a formula to include the factors like (i) average number of words in a sentence and (ii) the number of "hard words" (defined as words of three or more syllables, in each 100 words of text) . He called his formula as "fog Index". It is as follows:

SP+PS X 4 = fog Index.

In this formula SP stands for the average sentence length . This figure is obtained by dividing the number of words in a passage of text by the number of its sentences. PS means the percentages of words of three or more syllables, that is polysyllables.

To find the " fog Index" of his manuscript, a writer marks out samples of approximately 100 words each, spaced evenly throughout the document. In counting these samples, he stops his count with the sentence that ends nearest to the 100-word total. He then divides the number of words in all the passage by the number of sentences. The result is the average sentence length. This figure is placed in the formula as the SP item. Next he counts the number of three syllable or more in each 100 words and substitutes this figure for PS in the formula. In counting these polysyllables, the writer does not count words which are capitalised, words which are combinations of short and easy words, like " book keeping", or verb forms raised to the three syllable level by adding "ed" or "es," like "Created". Gunning thinks that easy reading matter should have a "fog Index" of approximately nine. Finally he needs S.P. and P.S. and multiplies by 4. The result is the "fog Index" which corresponds to school grades.

The Flesch Formula:

The most widely used measure of readability is the formula developed by Rudolf Flesch[5]. To test Readability level, Flesch divided his formula into two parts. His reading ease score is worked out like this:

1.	Multiply the average sentence legnth by 1.015	- - -
2.	Multiply the number of syllables per 100 words by 0.846	- - -
3.	Add (1) and (2)	- - -
4.	Subtract this sum (No. 3) from	206.835
5.	The reading difficulty level is	- - -

The reading difficulty score, as derived from the use of this particular Flesch formula locates the writing on a scale ranging from 0 to 100. At the top, the language is easy for any literate reader. A reading ease scoring table will be helpful in evaluating the difficulty of the languages.

Reading Ease Score	School Grade level	Readibility
90 to 100	4 th	Very easy
80 to 90	5 th	Easy
70 to 80	6 th	Fairly easy
60 to 70	7th or 8th	Standard
50 to 60	Some high school	Fairly difficult
30 to 50	High school	Difficult
20 to 30	Some college	Very difficult
0 to 20	College	Highly difficult

Flesch's second formula provided an Interest Index. His human Interest score is worked out like this:

a) Multiply the number of "personal words" per 100 words y 3.635 - - -
b) Multiply the number of"personal sentences" per 100 sentences by .314 - - -
c) add(1) and (2) - - -
d) The human Interest score is - - -

In using the human interest formula, a writer should bear in mind that personal words are all first, second, and third person pronouns and all words that have masculine or feminine gender. Personal sentences are spoken sentences marked by quotation marks, questions, commands, requests and other words directly addressed to the reader including exclamations and grammatically incomplete sentences just as in the case of the reading ease score. The Flesch Human Interest Index locates the writing on a scale ranging from zero (dull) to 100 (dramatic). Flesch described the style indicated by his Index as follows :

Human Interest Score	Description of style.
60 to 100.	Dramatic
40 to 60	Highly interesting.
20 to 40	Interesting
10 to 20	Mildly interesting
0 to 100	Dull

In 1954 flesch issued a new formula in his book(How to make sense) by simplifying the mathematical technique for gauging the ease with which people read. The new formula includes the counting of all "specific words" such as personal words, numbers dates and names, as well as the number of punctuation marks in every 100 words. Although this formula has interest to specialists in readability, the report writer will use it to test readability. On the basis of this formula, General Motors Corporation developed the reading ease calculator published by science research associates.

4.1.2 Methodology Followed :

From the review of related literature, it is found that the general purpose readability measures of Robort Gunning and Rudolf flesch are objective measures of comprehensing[6]. By using these measures, one can know the state of readability of a text and steps can be taken to modify the printed matters to suit the needs of relevant audience.In this endeavour, the readability of corporate annual reports of MPSLPEs has been evaluated by using the Rudolf flesch formula. The formula has been selected on the following considerations.

1. It is comparatively easy to apply.

2. It has been used in earlier studies in assessing readability of annual report by Soper and Dolphin[7], Barnett and Leoffer[8], R.C. Sharma[9],etc. In India Dr. R.C. Sharma has used this formula for assessing the readability of central level public enterprises. Hence, the Rundolf Flesch's formula[10] makes the study comparable with similar studies.

The Rudolf Flesch readability measure is shown by way of a formula as below :

$$\text{Reading difficult level score} = 206.835 - \frac{(\text{No.of words} \times 1.015}{(\text{No. of sentences}} + \frac{(\text{No.of syllables} \times 0.846 \times 100)}{\text{No. of words})}$$

By using the formula, various scores are derived and put in the table given below:

Formula score	School grade leve	Readability Measures	Characteri-stistic Score %
0-10	Post graduate	Most difficult	——
10-20	Some post graduate	Highly difficult	——
20-30	Post graduate	Very difficult	——
30-40	Some graduate	Difficult	——
40-50	Graduate	Fairly difficult	——

50-60	Higher secondary	Standard	——
60-70	Secondary	High standard	——
70-80	8th	Fairly easy	——
80-90	6th or 7th.	Easy	——
90-100	5th	Very easy.	——

After evaluating the aggregate position of readability, an attempt has been made to evalute the readability of the corporate report by dividing it into three major segments (as was done in earlier chapter)i.e.(i) Directors' report (ii) Auditors' report and (iii) Notes on accounts and foot notes. The necessary data (They are number of words, number of sentences and number of syllables) for each individual corporate report and its segments were obtained from the selected sampled paragraphs for readability computation of the reports.

(i). Directors'Report : Directors' report is the most informative and important part of the corporate annual report. It contains the significant information concerning to all sphere of activities of an enterprise. It is also widely used by the readers.IT is the lengthiest portion of the report. Therefore, a large sample was considered as appropriate. Three paragraphs each from begining, middle and end of the report were drawn.

(ii). Auditors' Report : The first paragraphs of the report of different PEs was found almost uniform. Therefore, a representative sample proportionate to the length of report of individual SLPE was drawn from the middle of the report.

(iii). Foot Notes and Notes on Account : There are wide variations in the number of notes in the corporate reports of individual PE. Hence, in some cases all notes available in the corporate report were considered. In other cases, a representative sample was drawn.

(iv). Annual report : For evaluation of readabiltity of corporate reports, the samples drawn for evaluation the readability of the three major segments were taken into account for obtaining the necessary data.

4.2 Readability Position of Corporate Report :

In this section, an attempt has been made to analyse the readability scores of individual SLPEs, average readability score and its variations.

4.2.1 Readabiltiy Scores of IndividualMPSLPEs :

By using Flesch formula for individual MPSLPEs, readability scores of selected MPSLPEs have been computed. The scores of Directors report, Auditors report and notes an account are shown in exhibit No. 4.1.

EXHIBIT No. 4.1

Readability scores of Individual Corporate Report and its three major segments

Name of Enterprise	Readability score: Directors' report	Auditors' report	Footnote & notes on Account	Aggregate (Annual report)
1. Agro Industries Development corporation	54.57	32.27	43.30	49.34
2. Forest Development Corporation	51.50	58.92	67.63	58.65
3. Small Industries Development Corporation				
4. Urja Vikas Nigam (EDC)	36.94	11.17	63.57	32.53
6. Police Housing Corporation	36.26	27.45	44.27	35.51
7. Seeds and Farms Development Corporation	37.11	65.65	51.50	51.46
8. Industrial Development Corporation	40.01	48.89	60.40	49.33
9. State Industires Corporation	36.69	47.21	72.32	51.38
10. State Road Transport Corporation	43.61	38.47	56.39	45.15
11. Fisheries development Corporation	38.44	37.81	40.33	40.23
12. Electronic Development Corporation	54.55	48.12	59.95	42.81
13. Land Development Corporation	41.82	33.65	52.38	44.19
14. Textile Corporation	39.53	26.90	70.13	46.83
15. Setu Nirman (BCC)	28.78	27.28	36.27	30.17
16. Nagarik Apurti Nigam	24.18.	23.74	27.47	25.75
17. Electricity Board	47.41	30.25	41.45	39.75
18. Tourism Development corporation.	43.74	20.16	35.54	38.42

Source : Compiled and computed from the data shown in theannual reports of the MPSLPEs.

4.2.2 Average Readability Score and its Variations :

The average readability scores and variations in the scores of the corporate reports and its components i.e. Directors' report, Auditors' report and Foot notes and notes on account have been computed. The scores have been shown in exhibit No. 4.2

EXHIBIT No. 4.2

Average Readability Score and its Variations

Name of Enterprise	Readability score Directors' report	Auditors' report	Footnote & notes on Account	Aggregate (Annual report)
Average readability score (X)	41.57	34.78	52.61	42.48
Range :				
Lowest score	24.18	11.17	27.48	25.76
Highest score	60.59	65.65	72.32	58.65
Co-efficient of range	0.43	0.71	0.45	0.39
Standard deviation	9.15	13.81	13.00	6.90
Co-efficient of variation	22.01	39.75	24.71	16.23
Easy readability positions	III	IV	I	II
Variations in ascending order	II	IV	III	I
Reading difficulty level	Fairly difficult	Difficult difficult	Standard	Fairly
School grade level.	Graduate	A few graduates	High school	Graduate

Source : Compiled and Computed from the figures shown in the annual reports of the MPSLPEs and exhibit No.4.1.

(i) The average readability score of 42.48 of the corporate reports indicates that the contents of the reports are fairly difficult to read and underst by a common man. However, educated persons at the graduate level can easily read and understand the message. The readability is difficult because writer has used difficult language, long and complex sentences and long words.

(ii) The readability score of individual corporate report in the selected MPSLPEs varies between 25.76 and 58.65. The standard deviation of 6.90 and co-efficient of variation of 16.23 indicates wide variations in the readability of the report.

This shows that some of the corporate bodies have made efforts to present their annual report in simple way and can be readable by a common person. However, some corporate entities have yet not made efforts towards this important aspect of annual reports.

(iii) The average readabilty score of Directors' report of selected MPSLPEs is 41.57. If we measure this score at reading difficult level, it shows that the readability is difficult and a person of graduate level can read and understand the message easily. It indicates that the most of the portion of Directors' report is written by using multisyllable complex and long sentences coupled with long words.

(iv) The readability score of the Directors' report varies between 24.18 and 60.59. The standard deviation of 9.15 and co-efficient of variation of 22.01 shows wide variations in the readability of the reports of MPSLPEs. It indicates that the some corporate entities have considered the readability and communication feature of the reports. However, a few of them have yet to take the initiatives.

(v) The average readability score of auditors report is 34.18. On the scale of difficult level and school grade level.it is measured as very difficult to read and understand. However, the contents can be read and understood by some of graduates. It indicates that writing style of the audit report is very complex and use of difficult language with long and complex sentences, and specific words which are not a part of common language.

(vi) The readability scores of audit reports varies between 11.17 to 65.65. The scores have standard deviation of 13.81 and co-efficient of variation of 39.72. This indicates wide variations in the readability score of the reports. This shows that some of the auditors write their report in plain language with simple sentences and common words whereas others are using uncommon language and complex presentation.

vii) The average readability score of notes on account and foot notes is found 52.61. It shows a standard level of presentation and higher secondary school grade person can easily read and grasp the message. Thus,the notes on accounts and foot notes have been written by using plain words and simple sentences.

(viii) The readability score of notes on account and foot notes varies between 27.47 and 72.32. The standard deviation is 13.0 and co-efficient of variation is 24.71. It shows wide variations.

(ix) If we look at three segments of annual report,. we find that easiest readability level is of notes on account. On the other hand, the most difficult readability level is found of auditors report.

4.2.3. Readability Position of Individual Corporate Report and its Segments :

Readability score of individual corporate report and its individual corporate report and its segments have been placed at "the reading difficult scoring table" in order to find the position of readability of the MPSLPEs. The readability position of report and segments have been shown in exhibit No. 4.3.

The readability position of individual report at the reading difficult scoring table revealed the following results :

(i) The readability scores of the majority of SLPEs (14 representing 77.77%of aggregate) have varied between 30 and 50 percent. This shows that these annual reports are difficult to read and are also difficult to understand. It is also clear from the table that only graduate person can follow the message comfortably.

(ii) In case of three SLPEs (16.67%) of the total), the readability score has varied between 50 and 60. This is the high standard level and person having higher secondary qualification can read easily and understand the message.

(iii) It is clear from the exhibit that the readability scores of these SLPEs has not exceeded 60%. This shows that there is greater scope of making these reports easier. It is also found that the readability score has not gone below 20%.

(iv) Regarding Directors' report, the trends were almost similar. The readability of twelve MPSLPEs was found at difficult level. In case of one MPSLPE, a person upto high school can easily understand.

(v) In case of audit report the distribution is more scattered. The difficulty level has also gone up. The readability has varied between 10% and 70%. Majority of MPSLPEs (12 constituting 66% of the total) have the readability score varying between

20 and 40. The scope of simplification is much higher in this case.

(vi) In case of foot notes and notes on account, the distribution is more dispersed. The readability has varied between 20 and 90. The difficult level has gone down. Even a person with higher secondary qualification can understand and the read the message in case of twelve SLPEs. In case of two SLPEs, the readability level is fairly easy.

4.3 Readability and Its Relationship withCompany Characteristics

The readability of a Corporate report may be affected by a number of company characteristics. In this section, an attempt has been made to examine the relationship of the readability of corporate report with the age of the enterprise, size of employment, rate of return, rate of turnover, size of enterprise in terms of capital employed and gross turnover. These characteristics have been examined on the following considerations :

(i) Age of Enterprise :

It is assumed that as firm grows in age, its report writing and presentation ability would improve. It is also assumed that aged firm would have involvement of people all walks of life having different levels of skill and ability.They will demand easy readability and understandable annual report.

(ii) Gross turnover :

Companies having larger gross turnover would have large and complex marketing system. Many common levels of people would have involvement in such a system. This may demand simple and readable corporate report. On the other hand, complexity would call for writing a report in specific terms which may make the report difficult to read and understand.

(iii) Rate of Raturn :

It is assumed that the companies which have higher rate of return on investment can employ highly skilled and experienced personnel for drafting and writing the corporate report. Therefore, the high rate of return of companies may publish easy and readable corporate reports. High rate of return of a company may induce us to show the profitability of the firm to the citizens and stakeholders. Therefore, the management may try to show in simple, easy and common language.

EXHIBIT No. 4.3

School Grade Level and Reading Difficult level of the Annual Reports

(Segmentwise break up)

Readibility score	School grade level	Readability level	No. of corporations and their percentage to sample							
			Aggregate		Directors report		Audit report		Footnote and notes on accounts	
			No.	%	No.	%	No.	%	No.	%
00-10	Post graduate (specified skill)	Most difficult	-	-	-	-	-	-	-	-
10-20	Some post graduate	High difficult	-	-	-	-	1	5.56	-	-
20-30	Post graduate	Very difficult	1	5.56	2	11.11	7	38.89	1	5.56
30-40	Some graduates	Difficult	6	33.33	7	38.88	5	27.78	2	11.11
40-50	Graduate	Fairly Difficult	8	44.44	5	27.78	3	16.67	4	22.22
50-60	Higher secondary (10+2)	High standard	3	16.67	3	16.67	1	5.56	5	27.78
60-70	High school	Standard	-	-	1	5.56	1	5.55	4	22.22
70-80	8th Middle	Fairly easy	-	-	-	-	-	-	1	5.56
80-90	6th of 7th	Easy	-	-	-	-	-	-	1	5.56
90-100	5th	Very easy	-	-	-	-	-	-	-	-
			18	100.00	18	100.00	18	100.00	18	100.00

Source: Compiled and computed from the figures shown in the annual report of the MPSLPEs

(iv) Capital Employed :

It is percieved that the company having large capital outlay would have mechanical system of preparation which may facilitate the modification of the written and printed matters to suit the appropriate audience. On the other hand, larger capital employed company would have complex production, marketing and accounting system which may involve technical language and use of specific terms which may be difficult to read and understand.

(v) Rate of Turnover :

Here, an attempt has been made to examine the effects of rate of turnover per hundered rupees of capital employed. It has been assumed that higher rate of turnover firm would have more facilities to make effective presentation of corporate report. Therefore, the readability of their annual reports would be easier than the in low rate of turnover firms.

(vi) Employment :

It is expected that the larger employment in an organisation would have sufficient manpower which would demand easy readable and understandable report. It would also have more number of skilled persons for report drafting, writing and persenting in effective form and to modify the text according to the requirements of the audience.

The relationship among the variables is conceptualised as follows:

$$Q = f\,(A, T, Rr, Ce, Rt, E)$$

'Q' denotes quality of readability. The A, T, Rt, Ce, Rt, and E repersents Age, Turnover, Rate of return,Capital employed, Rate of turnover and Employment respectively. While examining the relationship, the quality of the readability has been assumed as dependant variable and others are assumed as independent. It has also been assumed that other variables remain constant while examining the relationship between two variables. The `t' test has been used to determine the siqnificace of co-efficient of correlation. The computed `t' value has been compared with table value at 5% and 1% levels of significance at (N-2) degrees of freedom. Various hypotheses were formulated and they were tested to find out the relationship between the company characteristics and quality of readability of the annual reports as a whole as well between in each (i.e. Directors report, Audit report and Footnotes and Notes on accounts) segment of the report.

4.3.1: Readability of Corporate Report and Company Characteristics

In this section, the overall readability of corporate report and its relationship with company variables has been established by formulating and testing of null hypothesis H_o^{45} to H_o^{50} and the summary results have been shown in exhibit No. 4.4.

EXHIBIT No 4.4

Summary Results of Relationship of Readability of Annual Report with Company Characteristics

	Company Characteristics					
Particulars	**Age**	**Turn over**	**Rate of Return**	**Capital Employed**	**Rate of Turnover**	**Employment**
Coefficient of Correlation (r)	0.381	-0.300	0.2347	-0.124	0.149	-0.066
Value of "t"	1.648	1.257	0.683	0.499	0.583	0.231
Degrees of freedom (N-2)	16	16	8	16	15	11
Table value of "t":						
At 5% Significant level	2.120	2.120	2.306	2.120	2.731	2.201
At 1% Significant level	2.921	2.921	3.355	2.921	2.947	3.106
Hypothesis (H_o)	H^{45}_0	H^{46}_0	H^{47}_0	H^{48}_0	H^{49}_0	H^{50}_0
Result of Null hypothesis	A	A	A	A	A	A
Degree of correlation observed	LOW	LOW	LOW	LOW	LOW	LOW

Source : Computed from the information shown in the annual reports of selected MPSLPEOs

(i) Age of Enterprise and Quality of Readability of Corporate Report

Here an attempt has been made to examine the relationship between the age of the enterpirse and quality of readability of Corporate report by formulating and testing the following null hypothesis:

H_o^{45} : The Age of an enterprise and the quality of readability of corporate report are not related to each other.

The exhibit shows that the value of co-efficient of correlation +0.381 shows positive and low relationship. The computed value of "t" (18-2)=16 degrees of freedom is 1.648 which is less than table value of 't' at 2.120. Hence, the null hypothesis is accepted . Thus, it shows that the age of the enterprise and quality of readability of annual report are not related to each other.

(ii) Gross Turnover and Quality of Readability of Corporate Report

In this sub section, an attempt has been made to evaluate the relationship between gross turnover and quality of readability of corporate report by formulating and testing the null hypothesis as follows:

H_o^{46} : Gross turnover of enterprise does not influence the quality of readability of annual report.

The value of 'r' is (-0.300) which shows low degree of negative relationship. The computed value of 't' is 1.257 < 2.120 and 2.921 at 5% and 1% significant level respectively at (n-2) =16 degrees of freedom. The computed value of't' is less than the table values both at 5% and 1% significance level. Hence, the null hypothesis is accepted. Thus it shows that the gross turnover of enterprise does not have significent relationship with quality of readability of annual reports.

(iii) Rate of Return on Capital Employed and Quality of Readability of Corporate Report

We have tried to test the relationship between rate of return and quality of readability by formulating and testing the following null hypothesis:

H_o^{47} : Rate of return on Capital employed does not influence the readability of Corporate report.

The value of 'r' is .+0.235 which shows positive and low degree of relationship. The computed value of 't' is 0.683 which is less than the table values of 2.306 and 3.355 at 5% and 1% level of significance respectively at (18-2) = 16 degrees of freedom. Therefore, the null hypothesis is accepted. Hence, the rate of return on capital employed does not effect the quality of readability of corporate report.

(iv) Capital Employed and Quality of Readability of Corporate Report

We have tried to find out the relationship between the Capital employed in an organisation and quality of readability of corporate report. The following null hypothesis has beeen formulated and tested in this regard.

H_o^{48} : Size of enterprise in terms of capital employed and quality of readability of corporate report are not related to each other.

The value of 'r'(-0.124) shows low and negative relationship between the variables. From the exhinit No. 4.4 we find that the calculated value of 't' is 0.499 <2.120 and 2.921 at 5% and 1% level of significance respectively at (18 -2)=16 degrees of freedom. The value of 't' is less than the table values at both 5% and 1% level of significance, Hence, the null hypothesis is accepted. Thus, the size of capital employed and quality of readability of annual reports are not significantly related to each other.

(v) Rate of Turnover and Quality of Readability of Corporate Reports:

Here, the association between rate of turnover and quality of readability have been examined by formulating and testing the following null hypothesis:

H_o^{49} : Rate of turnover and quality of readability are not related to each other.

The value of 'r' is 0.149. It shows positive and low degree of relationship between the variables. The calculated value of't' is 0.583 which is less than the table values at 2.731 and 2.947 at 5% and 1% levels of significance respectively at (17-2)=15 degrees of freedom. Hence, the null hypothesis is accepted. Thus, it indicates that the rate of turnover and quality of readability of annual reports are not related significantly to each other.

(vi) Employment in the Enterprise and Readability of Corporate Annual Reports

The relationship between size of employment in terms of number of employees and quality of readability of annual reports have been examined by formulating and testing the following null hypothesis:

H_o^{50}: Size of employment in an organisation does not influence the quality of readability of corporate report.

The value of 'r' is (-0.066) which indicates negative and very low relationship between the variables. The calculated value of 't' is 0.231 which is less than the table values of 2.201 and 3.106 at 5% and 1% level of significance respectively at (13-2)=11 degrees of freedom. Hence, the null hypothesis is accepted. The size of employment in terms of number of employees in an enterprise does not have significant effect on the quality of readability of annual reports.

4.3.2 Readability of Directors Report and Company Characteristics:

We have made an attempt to examine the relationship between each company attribute and quality of readability of Directors report. The null hypothesis from H_0^{51} to H_0^{56} have been formulated and tested to find the relationship. The summary results have been shown in exhibit No.4.5.

EXHIBIT No. 4.5

SummaryResults of Directors Reports Readability and its Relationship with Company Characteristics

	Company Characteristics					
Particulars	**Age**	**Turn over**	**Rate of Return**	**Capital Employed**	**Rate of Turnover**	**Employment**
Coefficient of Correlation (r)	0.272	-0.04	-0.051	0.520	-0.607	-0.049
Value of "t"	1.131	0.158	0.144	2.435	2.959	0.1640
Degrees of freedom (N-2)	16	16	8	16	15	11
Table value of "t":						
At 5% Significant level	2.120	2.120	2.306	2.120	2.731	2.201
At 1% Significant level	2.921	2.921	3.355	2.921	2.947	3.106
Hypothesis (H_0)	H^{51}_0	H^{52}_0	H^{53}_0	H^{54}_0	H^{55}_0	H^{56}_0
Result of Null hypothesis	A	A	A	A	A	A
Degree of correlation observed	LOW	V.LOW	V.L.	V.H.	V.H.	V.L.

Source: Computed from the figures shown in the annual reports of selected MPSLPEs

(i) Age of enterprise and the readability of Directors report :

The association of age and quality of readability of Directors report has been examined by formulating and testing the following null hypothesis.

H_0^{51} : Age of an enterprise does not effect the quality of readability of Directors report.

The value of 'r' +0.272 shows positive and low degree of relationship.The calculated value of 't'is 1.131 which is less than table values of 2.210 and 2.921 at 5% and 1% level of significance respectively at (18-2)=16 degrees of freedom. The computed value of 't' is less than both 5% and 1% level of significance. Hence, null hypothesis is accepted. Thus, the age of an enterprise does not influence the quality of readability of Directors report significantly.

(ii) Gross Turnover and Quality of Readability of Directors Reports

We have tried to find the influence of gross turnover on quality of readability of Directors' report by testing the following null hypothesis:

H_o^{52} : Gross turnover in the enterprise does not influence the quality of readability of Directors' report.

The value of 'r' (-0.040) shows very low and negative relationship between turnover and readability of Directors' report. The calculated value of 't' 0.158 which is less than the table values of 2.120 and 2.921 at 5% and 1% level of significance respectively at (18-2)=16 degrees of freedom. Hence, the null hypothesis is accepted. Thus, the relationship between turnover and quality of readability of Directors' report are not significantly related to each other.

(iii) Rate of Return and Quality of Readability of Directors' Report

The influence of rate of return on capital employed has been examined by formulating and testing the following null hypothesis:

Ho^{53}: Rate of return on capital employed and quality of readability of Directors' report are not related to each other.

The value of 'r' is (-0.051) which is very low and shows negative relationship between the variables. The computed value of 't' is 0.144. It is less than the table value of 2.306 and 3.355 at 5% and 1% level of significance respectively at (18-2)=16 degrees of freedom. Hence, the null hypothesis is accepted. It shows that the rate of return on capital employed has no influence on the quality of readability of Directors' report.

(iv). Capital Employed and Readability of Directors' Report:

The relationship between capital employed and quality of readability of Directors report has been tested by formulating and testing the null hypothesis as follows :

H_o^{54} : The size of an enterprise in terms of Capital employed does not have influence on quality of readability of Directors' report.

The exhibit shows that the value of "r" 0.520 shows the positive and high degree of relationship between the variables. The computed value of "t" is 2.435 which is greater than the value at 2.120 at 5% level of significance. But it is less than 2.921 at 1% level of significance. Thus, the null hypothesis is rejected at 5% level of significance at (18-2)=16 degrees of freedom. Hence, it shows significance influence of size of capital employed on quality of readability of Directors' report.

(v). Rate of Turnover and Readability of Directors' Report

The relationship between rate of turnover and readability of Directors' report has been examined by formulating and testing the null hypothesis as follows :

H_o^{55} : Rate of turnover and quality of readability of Directors' report are not related to each other.

The value of "r" (-0.607) shows negative and high degree of correlationship between the variables. The computed value of "t"is 2.959 > 2.731 and 2.947 at 5% and 1% level of significance respectively at (17-2)=15 degrees of freedom. Since the computed value of "t" is greater than tabular values both at 5% and 1% levels of significance, the null hypothesis is rejected. It is found that rate of turnover and quality of readability of Directors'report are significantly corelated to each other.

(vi) Employment and Quality of Readability of Directors' Report

The readability of Directors report and its relationship with size of employment in terms of number of employees in the enterprise has been examined by formulating and testing the null hypothesis as follows :

H_o^{56} : Size of employment in an organization does not influence the quality of readability of Directors report.

The value of "r" (-0.049) shows negative relationship. The computed value of 't' is 0.164 < 2.201 and 3.106 at 5% and 1% levels of significance respectively at (13-2)=11 degrees of freedom. Thus, the null hypothesis is accepted. It is found that size of employment does not have significant influence on quality of readability of Directors' report.

4.3.3. Readability of Auditors Report and Company Characteristics:

In ths section, an attempt has been made to find the relationship between readability of auditors report and company attributes. The null hypothesis numbered from H_0^{57} to H_0^{62} have been formulated and tested in this connection. The summary results have been shown in exhibit No. 4.6.

EXHIBIT No. 4.6

Summary Results of Readability of Audit Report and its Relationship with Company Characteristics

	Company Characteristics					
Particulars	**Age**	**Turn over**	**Rate of Return**	**Capital Employed**	**Rate of Turnover**	**Employment**
Coefficient of Correlation (r)	-0.068	-0.129	-0.409	-0.71	0.436	0.517
Value of "t"	0.272	0.519	1.269	0.283	1.875	2.005
Degrees of freedom (N-2)	16	16	8	16	15	11
Table value of "t":						
At 5% Significant level	2.120	2.123	2.306	2.120	2.731	2.201
At 1% Significant level	2.921	2.921	3.355	2.921	2.947	3.106
Hypothesis (H_0)	H^{57}_0	H^{58}_0	H^{59}_0	H^{60}_0	H^{61}_0	H^{62}_0
Result of Null hypothesis	A	A	A	A	A	A
Degree of correlation observed	HIGH	V.L.	HIGH	LOW	LOW	LOW

Source : Computed from the figures shown in the annual reports of the selected MPSLPEs.

(i) Age of Enterprise and Quality of Readability of Audit Report :

We have tried to examine the relationship between age of enterprise and quality of readability of audit report by formulating and testing the null hypothesis as follows :

H_0^{57} : Age of enterprise and quality of readability of Audit report are not related to each other.

The exhibit shows that the value of "r" (-0.068) shows negative relationship between the attributes. The calculated `t' value of 0.272 is less than table values of 2.120 and 2.921 at 5% and 1% level of significance respectively at (18-2)= 16 degrees of freedom. Hence, the null hypothesis is accepted. Thus the age of enterprise does not have significant influence on quality of readability of audit report.

(ii) Gross Turnover and Quality of Readability of Audit Report

It has been tried to examine the ralationship between gross turnover and quality of readability of Audit report by formulating and testing the null hypothesis as follows.

H_o^{58} : Gross turnover of the enterprise and quality of readability ofaudit report are not related to each other.

The value of "r" is (-0.129) which shows negative and low degree of relationship. The calculated value of "t" is 0.519. It is less than the table values of 2.123 and 2.921 at 5% and 1% level of significance respectively at (18-2)=16 degrees of freedom. Threfore, the null hypothesis is accepted. It is found that gross turnover does not have significant influence on quality of readability of audit report.

(iii) Rate of Return and Readability of Audit Report

Here, an attempt has been made to examine relationship of the readability of Audit report with the rate of return by formulating and testing the following null hypothesis :

H_o^{59} : Rate of return does not influence the quality of readability of audit report.

The value of "r" (-0.409) shows negative and fairly high relationship between the variables. The computed value of "t" is 1.269 at (10-2)=8 degrees of freedom which is less than the table values of 2.3069 and 3.355 at 5% and 1% level of significance. Hence, the null hypothesis is accepted. Therfore, it is found that rate of return does not have effected the quality of readability of audit report.

(iv). Size of Capital Employed and Readability of Audit Report

The association between size of Capital employed and quality of readability of Audit report has been examined. The null hypothesis formulated and tested in this regard is as follows :

H_o^{60} : Size of an enterprise in terms of capital employed does not influnece the quality of readability of Audit report.

The value of "r" is found at (-0.071). It indicates negative and low degree of relationship between the variables. The calculated value of "t" at 0.283 is less than the table values of 2.120 and 2.921 at 5% and

1% level of significance and at (18-2)=16 degrees of freedom. Hence, the null hypothesis is accepted. It shows that the size of capital employed does not have significant influence on quality of readability of Audit report.

(v). Rate of Turnover and Readability of Audit Report

Rate of turnover and its effect on quality of readability of audit report has been evaluated by formulating and testing the following null hypothesis :

H_o^{61} : Rate of turnover of a company does not influence the readability of audit report.

The exhibit shows that the value of "r" is 0.436. It shows high degree of relationship between variables. The computed value of "t" is 1.8575 < 2.731 and 2.947 at 5% and 1% level of significance at(17-2)=15 degrees of freedom. Thus,the null hypothesis is accepted. It shows that the rate of turnover of the companies does not have significant influence on the quality of readability of audit report.

(vi). Size of Employment and the Readability of Audit Report

We have made an effort to examine the relationship between size of employment and the quality of audit report. The following null hypothesis has been formulated and tested in this regard:

H_o^{62} : Size of employemnt does not influence the quality of readability of Audit report.

The value of "r" is 0.517.It shows that high degree of positive relationship between the variables. The computed value of "t" at 2.005 is less than the table values of 2.202 and 3.106 at 5% and 1% level of significance at (13-2)=11 degrees of freedom. Hence, the null hypothesis is accepted. It shows that the employment in terms of number of employees does not have significant influence on the quality of readability of audit report.

4.3.4 Readability of Notes on Account and Footnotes and Company Characteristics :

The relationship between the readability of notes on accounts and footnotes and each company charecteristics have been examined. The null hypothesis numbered from H_o^{63} to H_o^{68} were formulated and tested. The summary results have been shown in exhibit No 4.7.

EXHIBIT No. 4.7

Summary Results of Readability of Footnotes and Notes on Account and its Associationship with Company Characteristics

	Company Characteristics					
Particulars	**Age**	**Turn over**	**Rate of Return**	**Capital Employed**	**Rate of Turnover**	**Employment**
Coefficient of Correlation (r)	0.255	-0.294	0.369	-0.175	0.311	-0.149
Value of "t"	1.054	1.233	-01.122	0.712	1.453	0.152
Degrees of freedom (N-2)	16	16	8	16	15	1[illegible]
Table value of "t":						
At 5% Significant level	2.120	2.123	2.306	2.120	2.731	2.201
At 1% Significant level	2.921	2.921	3.355	2.925	2.947	3.106
Hypothesis (H_0)	H^{63}_0	H^{64}_0	H^{65}_0	H^{66}_0	H^{67}_0	H^{58}_0
Result of Null hypothesis	A	A	A	A	A	A
Degree of correlation observed	LOW	LOW	LOW	LOW	LOW	LOW

Source : Computed from figures shown in the annual reports of selected MP'SLPEs

(i). Age of the Enterprise and Readability of Notes on Accounts and Footnotes :

To find out the relationship between these two variables the following null hypothesis has been formulated and tested :

H_0^{63} : Age of the enterprise and the quality of readability of foot notes and notes on accounts are not related to each other.

The exhibit shows that the value of "r" is 0.255. It shows positive relationship between variables. The computed value of "t" at 1.054 is less than the tabular values both 2.120 and 2.921 at 5% and 1% level of significance, at (18-2)=16 degrees of freedom. Hence,the null hypothesis is accepted. It shows that the age of the enterprise does not have significant influence on quality of readability of notes on accounts and foot notes.

(ii). Gross Turnover and Readability of Notes on Accounts and Foot Notes

An attempt has been made to evaluate the influence of gross turnover on the quality of readability of notes on accounts and foot notes. The following null hypothesis has been formulated and tested :

H_o^{64} : Turnover of an enterprise and quality of readability of notes on accounts and foot notes are not related to each other.

The value of "r" is (-0.294). It shows negative low degree of relationship. The "t" value of 1.233 is less than table values of 2.120 and 2.921 at 5% and 1% level of significance respectively at (18-2)=16 degrees of freedom. Hence, the null hypothesis is accepted. Therefore, the turnover does not have significant influence on the quality of readability of notes on accounts and foot notes.

(iii). Rate of Return and the Readability of Notes on Accounts and Foot Notes

The association between these two variables have been examined by formulating and testing the following null hypothesis:

H_o^{65} : Rate of return on capital employed does not influence the quality of readability of notes on accounts and foot notes.

The value of "r" is 0.369. It shows positive and low degree of relationship between the variables. The computed value of "t" is 1.122. It is less than the table values of 2.306 and 3.355 at 5% and 1% level of significance respectively at (18-2)=16 degrees of freedom. Hence,the null hypothesis is accepted. Thus it is found that rate of return on capital employed does not influence the quality of readability of notes on accounts and foot notes.

(iv) Capital Employed and Readability of Notes on Accounts and Foot Notes :

In this sub section, we have made an attempt to evaluate the relationship between capital employed and the quality of readability of notes on accounts and foot notes. The following null hypothesis has been formulated and tested.

H_o^{66} : Size of enterprise in term of capital employed and quality of readability of notes on accounts and foot notes are not related to each other.

The value of "r" is (-0.175). It shows negative relationship. The calculated value of "t" is 0.712 < 2.120 and 2.921 at 5% and 1% level of significance and at (17-2)=15 degrees of freedom. Hence,the null hypothesis is accepted. It is found that the size of capital employed does not have significant influence on quality of readability of notes on accounts and foot notes.

(v) Rate of Turnover and Readability of Notes on Account and Foot Notes.

We have made an effort to evalute the influence of rate of turnover on the quality of readability of notes on accounts and foot notes. The following null hypothesis is formulated and tested :

H_o^{67} : Rate of turnover of an enterprise does not influence the quality of readability of notes on accounts and foot notes.

The value of co-efficient of correlation 'r' is 0.311 which shows positive degree of relationship between the variables. The calculated value of 't' is 1.453. It is less than the tabular values of 2.731 and 2 947 at 5% and 1% level of significance at (17-2)=15 degrees of freedom. Hence,the null hypothesis is accepted. Thus, it indicates that the rate of turnover does not have significant effect on quality of readability of foot notes and notes on account.

(vi) Size of Employment and the Readability of Notes on Account and Foot Notes:

We have also made an attempt to examine the relationship between size of employment in terms of number of employees and quality of readability of notes on account. The following null hypothesis has been formulated and tested:

H_o^{68} : Size of employment does not effect the quality of readability of notes on accounts and foot notes.

The exhibit shows that the value of 'r' is (-0.149). It shows negative relationship between the variables. The computed value of 't' is 0.152<2.201 and 3.106 at 5% and 1% significance level respectively at (13-2)=11 degrees of freedom. Hence, the null hypothesis is accepted. Thus, it is found that the size of employment in terms of number of employees does not influence the quality of readability of notes on accounts and foot notes.

REFERENCES

1. Douglas Paul, *Communication Through Reports,* Prentice-Hall inc. Englewood Eliffs, N.J. 1965 p.7.
2. Klare, G. *The Measurement of Readability,* "Quoted in Corporate Reporting in Public Enterprises in India - by R.C. Sharma, "Financial Reporting in Public Enterprises" opcited, p.61.
3. R.C. Sharma, *Financial Reporting in Public Enterprises in India,* opcited, p.161.
4. Robert Gunning, *Techniques of Clear Writing,* opcited, pp.36-39.
5. Rudolf Flesch , *"How to test Readability",* opcited, p.6.
6. Paul Dugless, *Communication Through Report,* opcited p.51.
7. Soper,J.F. and Dolphin,R. *Readability and Corporate Annual Reports,* The Accounting Review, Vol.XXXVIII No.2,April 1963, p.362.
8. Bornett, A. and Leoffer, K., *Readability of Accounting and Auditing Messages* - The Journal of Business Communication, Vol.16 No.39,p.51.
9. Sharma R.C. "*Financial Reporting in Public Enterprises in India*" opcited pp.160-212.
10. Rudolf Flesch, *The Art of plain talk* Harper & Brothers, New York 1946, p.66.

5

CONCLUDING OBSERVATIONS

The disclosure of information in state level public enterprises is very scanty and delayed. The guidelines of the Bureau and State Government are usually flouted. The MPSLPEs are not an exception to this state of affairs. The present study of 18 MPSLPEs (universe-33) aims to evaluate the corporate reporting practices with reference to extent of disclosure, timeliness and readability. All information is collected from the published annual reports of the selected MPSLPEs. The latest available reports as on 31 March 1990 was scanned to extract the useful information for analysis. About 69 hypothesis were formulated to test the inter-relationship of various factors influencing the reporting practices of MPSLPEs. The analysis has been made by dividing the contents of annual reports into three parts; Directors' report, Accounting information and Voluntary information. The first two parts may be taken as Statutory information. In this chapter, an attempt has been made to narrate briefly the major findings of the study alongwith a suggestive framework for action.

5.1 Major Findings:

The main finding of the study are narrated briefly in this sub section.Finding were shown separately for each chapter.

5.1.1 Content Analysis and Extent of Information Disclosure:

The following are the main results of the investigation regarding content analysis and extent of information disclosure:

(i) The size in terms of pages of annual report varies between 29 (MPEDC) and 143 pages (MPIDC).

(ii) Majority of the MPSLPEs have published their annual reports, in both the languages - Hindi and English.

(iii) Only 12.50% of selected MPSLPEs have presented the information by using the sophisticated symbols viz. graphs, chart, etc. to convey the message.

(iv) The following are the some of the items and their disclosure percentage.

(a)	Future Prospects	37.50
(b)	Contribution to Environmental Protection	36.36
(c)	Conservation of Energy	18.75
(d)	Research and Development	46.67
(e)	Segment Reporting (Unit wise)	41.66
(f)	Social Overhead Accounting	31.25
(g)	Funds Flow Statement	25.00
(h)	Cash Flow Statement	0 %
(i)	Value Added Statement	0 %
(j)	Inflation Accounting	0 %
(k)	Human Assets Accounting	0 %
(l)	Accounting Policies	62.5
(m)	Historical Summaries of Selected Financial and Operational Statistics	50.0 %
(n)	Pictorial Presentation	12.50 %
(o)	Organisation Structure	31.25 %
(p)	Statement to Contribution to Exchequer	0 %
(r)	Social Accounting	0 %
(s)	Current Cost Accounting	0 %
(t)	Profitability Statement	0 %

(v) Details regarding the name, designation and tenure of Directors' is uniformally disclosed by all the MPSLPEs. The details regarding the notice and registered office are the statutory requirement of disclosure.

(vi) The size of Directors' report has varied from 2 to 14 pages. MPEDC, MPCSC, MPEB and MPFDC have attached the annexures to the Directors' report. The content of Directors' report differ in nature and quantity from one enterprise to another. The operating results, capital structure, operational activities, details about sales and marketing, research and development, personnel, organisation and management, accounting policies, information about the subsidiary companies, details of material changes and commitment, future prospects, etc. were shown by these selected SLPEs.

(vii) MPSLPEs have presented profit and loss account either in 'T' form or in statement form. The MPPHC, MPS & FDC, MPIDC, MPCSC and MPEDC have presented their profit and loss account in 'T' form. The detailed information about an item of profit and loss account has been provided by way of schedules. The number of schedules varies from one PE to another. The MPSEDC provides 14 schedules to its profit and loss account whereas MPEDC provides four schedules to its profit and loss account.

(viii) Balance sheet has been presented either in 'T' form or in vertical form. The MPSLPEs which have presented in 'T' form are MPFC, MPPHC and MPCSC. The MPSLPEs which present in vertical form includes MPSEDC, MPSIDC and MPAIDC. The schedules to the balance sheet varies between 5 and 16 in number.

(ix) Notes on account varies in number and size in MPSLPEs. The MPCSC shows 36 notes on account covering 5 pages whereas MPEDC gave 7 notes on account covering two pages. MPFDC gives 25 notes on account covering 7 pages.

(x) The MPSLPEs which have disclosed the contingent liabilities include MPSIC, MPSIDC, MPFDC and MPEDC. The MPSEDC have disclosed the contingent liabilities relating to outstanding bank guarantees, out standing letter of credit, indemenities for advance payments, claims of central government, excise department and outstanding bonds for customs duty.

(xi) Additional information in the form of accounting ratios, historical summaries of financial and operational statistics and funds flow statement are also disclosed by selected MPSLPEs.

(xii) The cash flow statement, ratios relating to liquidity and profitability, human resource accounting and value added statement, have not been disclosed by any MPSLPEs.

(xiii) There are 93.75% MPSLPEs which disclose more than 60% information in their annual reports. There are 37.50% MPSLPEs whose disclosure percentage is above 80%. Only 12.50% MPSLPEs are disclosing more than 90% of the information in their annual reports.

(xiv) The information disclosure in Directors' report by MPSLPEs is found between 30% and 100 %. There are 82.1% MPSLPEs which disclose more than 50% information. 31.25% of MPSLPEs disclose 80% to 90% information. There is only one MPSLPE which disclose more than 90% information in its Directors' report. The smallest disclosure percentage in Directors' report is found at 39.15% and the highest disclosure is found at 97.62%.

(xv) 93.25% of MPSLPEs disclose more than 70% of accounting information; 50% MPSLPEs disclose more than 80% and 31% of MPSLPEs disclose information ranging between 90% to 100%.

(xvi) The disclosure percentage of voluntary information varies between 16% and 72%. The 68.5% of MPSLPEs disclose less than 50% and 56.25% of MPSLPEs disclose less than 40% of voluntary information.

(xvii) The disclosure of information by sample units varies from 39.62% to 93.12%. The average disclosure of the units included in the sample is 74.16%. The disclosure position in three major segments of annual report is found as follows.

(i) Directors' Report:

Lowest disclosure	:	39.15%
Highest disclosure	:	97.62%
Average disclosure	:	68.04%

(ii) Accounting Information:

Lowest disclosure	:	41.00%
Highest disclosure	:	100.00%
Average disclosure	:	82.92%

(iii) Voluntary information:

Lowest disclosure	:	16.00%
Highest disclosure	:	72.00%
Average disclosure	:	40.25%

This reveals that the management of MPSLPEs is more concerned to the compulsory disclosure requirements of information.

(xviii) 92 items (42.79%) have been disclosed by ninety to hundred percent companies. 31 items (14.42%) have been disclosed by 80% to 90% companies and 19 items (8.84%) have been disclosed by more than 70% companies. 54 items (25.23%) have been disclosed by 0 to 50% companies and 161 (74.77%) items have been disclosed by 50% to 100% companies. The aggregate picture reveals that the management of some companies ignores the disclosure of some items of information in their annual reports.

(xix) Directors report of MPSLPEs shows wide variation in disclosure percentage of individual items. 26.42% of items have been disclosed by 90% to 100% companies. There are 60 to 70% items which have been disclosed by more than 20% companies. 30.19% items have been disclosed by 0 to 50% companies and 69.81% items have been disclosed 50% to 100% companies.

(xx) Voluntary items have also been disclosed by a few companies. There are 28.0% items which have been disclosed by 10.20% companies and there are only 8% items which have been disclosed by 90% to 100% companies.

(xxi) Effect of company characteristics viz. gross turnover, rate of return, size of capital employed, size of employment, age of enterprise and rate of turnover on the information disclosure in the annual report is found as follows -

(a) The 'r' between gross turnover and quantity of disclosure is 0.419. The calculated value of 't' is 1.725. It is less than the tabulated values of 2.145 at 5% level of significance and 2.977 at 1% level of significance for 14 degrees of freedom. This shows the acceptance of null hypothesis. This reflects that the gross turnover does not significantly influence the quantity of disclosure.

(b) The negative value of 0.098 with respect to 'r' between rate of return on investment and quantity of disclosure was evaluated by 't' test. The null hypothesis was accepted. This has shown the independance of two factors.

(c) The 't' test has also shown that the size of the enterprise and quantity of disclosure are independent to each other. The calculated value of 't' is 0.885. It is much less than the tabular values of more than 2.

(d) The null hypothesis to evaluate the impact of number of employees on quantity of disclosure was formulated for 't' test. The calculated value was 1.287 which is less than the tabular value. As the null hypothesis is accepted, the size of employment does not have significant impact on quantity of disclosure.

(e) The 'r' between age of enterprise and quantity of disclosure is 0.624. The computed value of 't' is 2.984 which is much higher than the tabular values. The null hypothesis was rejected and it was found that the older PEs disclose more information than the new PEs in their annual reports.

(xxii) Effect of company characteristics on quantity of disclosure in the Directors' report is examined by testing the following null hypothesis:

(a) The 'r' between turnover and quantity of disclosure in Directors' report is 0.545. The computed value of 't' is 2.435. It is higher than the tabular value of 2.145 at 5% level of significance. The null hypothesis was rejected and it was found that the turnover has significant effect on quantity of disclosures in Directors' report. In other words, the PEs with the higher turnover disclose more quantity of information than PEs with lower turnover.

(b) The negative value of 'r' between rate of returns and quantity of disclosure was 0.333. By using 't' test, the null hypothesis was accepted. This has shown the independance of two factors.

(c) The 't' test has also shown that size of enterprise and quantity of disclosure are not significantly associated with each other. The calculated value of 't' is 2.112. (the tabular value 2.160).

(d) The hypothesis to examine the impact of size of employment on quantity of disclosure in Directors' report was formulated and 't' test was used. The calculated value of 't' was 0.721 which is less than the tabular value of 3.250. The null hypothesis was accepted. Hence, the size of employment does not have significant impact on quantity of disclosure in Directors' report.

(e) The 'r' between age of enterprise and quantity of disclosure in Directors' report is 0.117. The computed value of 't' is 0.441. It is much less than the tabular values. The null hypothesis was accepted. It shows independance of two factors.

(xxiii) Effect of company characteristics on quantity of accounting information is examined by testing the following null hypothesis:

(a) The 'r' between gross turnover and quantity of Accounting Information is 0.427. The computed value of 't' is 1.765 at 5% level of significance at 14 degrees of freedom. The computed value is less than tabular values. This reflects that the gross turnover does not significantly influence the quantity of accounting information disclosure.

(b) The 'r' between rate of return and quantity of accounting information is (-.183). The computed value of 't' is 0.560. It is less than the tabular values. The null hypothesis is accepted. This shows that rate of return on investment does not influence the quantity of accounting information disclosure.

(c) By using the 't' test, the relationship between size of enterprise and quantity of accounting information disclosure shows the computed value of 't' at 1.238 (tabular value 2.160). This reveals that the size of enterprise in terms of capital employed does not influence the quantity of accounting information significantly.

(d) The hypothesis to test the impact of number of employees on quantity of disclosure in accounting information was tested on 't' scale. The calculated value was 1.447. It is less than the tabular values. As the null hypothesis is accepted, the size of employment does not have significant impact on quantity of accounting information disclosure.

(e) The 'r' between age of enterprise and quantity of accounting information disclosure is 0.579. The computed value of 't' is 2.560 at 5% level of significance at 14 degrees of freedom. The tabular value of 2.145 is less than computed value. Thus, the null hypothesis is rejected. It shows that the age of enterprise has significant impact on accounting information disclosure. The older PEs disclose more accounting information than new PEs.

(xiv) Effect of company characteristics on quantity of voluntary information disclosure is examined by formulating and testing the following null hypothesis:

(a) The 'r' between gross turnover and quantity of voluntary disclosure is 0.473. The calculated value of 't' is 2.000. It is less than the tabulated values of 2.145 at 5% level of significance and 2.977 at 1% level of significance for 14 degrees of freedom. This shows the acceptance of null hypothesis. This reflects that the gross turnover does not significantly influence the quantity of voluntary disclosure.

(b) The co-efficient of correlation between rate of return on investment and quantity of disclosure is 0.120. By using 't' table, the null hypothesis was accepted. This shows the independance of two factors.

(c) The 't' test has also shown that the size of enterprise and quantity of disclosure when tested are found, independant to each other. The calculated value of 't' is 0.248. It is much less than the tabular values.

(d) The hypothesis to assess the impact of number of employees on quantity of disclosure was formulated and 't' test was used. The calculated value was 0.760. It is less than the tabular values. As the null hypothesis is accepted, the size of employment does not have significant impact on quantity of disclosure.

(e) The 'r' between age of enterprise and quantity of disclosure is 0.653. The computed value of 't' is 3.229. It is much higher than the tabular values. The null hypothesis was rejected. In other words, the older SLPEs disclose more voluntary information than new SLPEs in their annual report.

5.1.2 Timeliness in Corporate Reporting:

Timely disclosure and presentation of information improves the image of the corporate body. It shows managerial efficiency and effectiveness. It reflects quickness in finalisation of accounts and their presentation. It enriches the relationship between management and user groups. The main findings regarding timeliness are narrated below:

(i) The audit time lag of individual SLPE varies between 60 and 2291 days. Average audit time lag is 1030.13 days. Half of the SLPEs has the audit time lag between 1500 and 2000 days.

(ii) It is also found that 8 annual reports out of 16 contain comments of C AGs. Their time lag varies between 11 and 224 days. However, 75% of MPSLPEs take 50 to 100 days time. The average time lag is 79.75 days.

(iii) The time taken by MPSLPEs in holding their annual general meeting after the completion of audit and C & AGs review varies between 22 and 295 days. The average reporting time lag is 95.60 days. However, 62.5% of the MPSLPEs take around 50 days time in holding the annual general meeting after completion of audit and review of C & AGs.

(iv) The time taken in holding annual general meeting from the date of last day of accounting year varies between 88 and 2520 days. The average time lag is 1139.88 days. 43.25% of the MPSLPEs take more than 1000 days to hold the annual general meeting. There are only 8 MPSLPEs which take 500 to 1000 days in holding annual general meeting.

(v) When we look at the variations, we find that the range of the audit lag is the highest. It has constituted 92% of the total lag. On the other hand, the C & AGs' reporting lag has an insignificant share varying between 3 and 5 percent. The co-efficient of range has not varied much. It clearly indicates that the variations in individual MPSLPEs are insignificant.

(vi) The company form of MPSLPEs takes more time to release their annual report than statutory and societies form of enterprises. Statutory form of MPSLPEs are disclosing the information earlier than the other two forms.

(vii) Effect of company characteristics viz. age, turnover, capital employed, rate of turnover, employment and rate of return on timeliness (Total time lag) in Corporate reporting in MPSLPEs is found as follows:

(a) The 'r' between age of enterprise and total time lag is (- 0.081). The calculated value of 't' is 0.325. It is less than tabulated values of 2.145 at 5% level of significance and 2.977 at 1% level of significance for 14 degrees of freedom. This shows the acceptance of null hypothesis. This reflects that the age of enterprise does not significantly influence the total time lag.

(b) The value of 'r' (- 0.158) between total time lag and gross turnover was tested by 't' test. The null hypothesis was accepted. This has shown the independance of two factors.

(c) The 't' test has also shown that the size of enterprise in terms of capital employed and total time lag are independant to each other. The calculated value of 't' is 0.452. It is much less than table value of 't' at 2.160.

(d) The null hypothesis to evaluate the impact of rate of turnover on total time lag was formulated. By using 't' test, the calculated value of 't' was found at 0.690 which is less than the tabular value of 2.160 at 13 degrees of freedom. Hence, the null hypothesis was accepted. The rate of turnover does not significantly influence the time lag.

(e) The value of 'r' between employment and total time lag was negative 0.159. By using 't' test, the value of 't' was ascertained at 0.455 at 8 degrees of freedom. It is less than the table values of 't' at 5% and 1% level of significance. This has shown the acceptance of null hypothesis. Thus, the number of employees in an enterprise does not influence the total time lag.

(f) The impact of rate of return on total time lag was evaluated by 't' test. The value of 't' was 0.956 at 9 degrees of freedom. It was less than the tabular values of 2.262 at 5% significance level and 3.250 at 1% level of significance. This has shown acceptance of null hypothesis at both the levels. Thus, the rate of return on capital employed does not have significance influence on time lag.

(viii) The effects of company characteristics on audit lag has been examined by testing the following null hypothesis:

(a) The value of 'r' (- 0.153) between the age of enterprise and audit lag was evaluated by using 't' test. The calculated value of 0.581 at 14 degrees of freedom was less than the table values at 5% and 1% level of significance. This shows that the age of enterprise does not influence the audit lag.

(b) The value of 'r' between audit lag and gross turnover was tested by using 't' test. The computed value was less than the table values of 't' at 5% and 1% level of significance. This shows that the gross turnover and audit lag are not related to each other.

(c) The null hypothesis was tested to find the relationship between capital employed and audit lag. The computed value of 't' was less than the tabular values. It was found that capital employed does not have significant impact on audit lag.

(d) The value of 'r' between rate of turnover and audit lag was 0.095 negative. By using 't' test, the computed value of 't' was found. It was less than the tabular values of 't'. Hence, the null hypothesis was accepted. This shows that the rate of turnover and audit lag are not related to each other.

(e) The impact of number of employees on audit lag was tested by 't' test. The computed value of 0.131 at 8 degrees of freedom was less than the table values at 5% and 1% level of significance. Hence, the null hypothesis was accepted. It shows that the size of employment does not have significant impact on audit lag.

(f) The coefficient of correlation between rate of return and audit lag was negative 0.316. The computed value of 't' was 0.999. This is less than the table values of 't' at 5% and 1% level of significance at 9 degrees of freedom. Hence, the null hypothesis was accepted. This has shown that rate of return and audit lag are not related to each other.

(ix) The effect of company characteristics on C & AGs time lag has been examined by testing the following null hypothesis:

(a) The coefficient of correlation between the age of enterprise and C & AGs' time lag was negative 0.161. It was tested by using 't' test. The null hypothesis was accepted as computed value was less than the tabular values of 't'. It has shown that age of enterprise does not influence the C & AGs' time lag.

(b) The null hypothesis was tested to find the relationship between gross turnover and C & AGs' time lag. The computed value of 't' was less than the table values at 5% and 1% levels of significance. The null hypothesis was accepted. The test shows that gross turnover and C&AGs' time lag are not related to each other.

(c) The impact of capital employed on C&AGs' time lag was evaluated by using 't' test. The computed value of 't' was less than the tabular values of 2.447 at 5% level and 3.707 at 1% level of significance at 6 degrees of freedom. It shows that the capital employed does not have significant impact on C & AGs time lag.

(d) The influence of rate of turnover on C &AG'stime lag was tested by 't' test. The computed value of 't' was less than table values. They are 2.447 at 5% level and 3.707 at 1% significance level. It shows that the rate of turnover and C&AGs time lag are not related to each other.

(e) The influence of number of employees on C&AG's time lag was tested by 't' test. The computed value was less than the table values. Hence, the null hypothesis was accepted. It is found that number of employees in an enterprise does not influence the C&AG's time lag.

(f) The value of 'r' between rate of return and C&AGs time lag was tested by using 't' test. The computed value of 't' was more than table values. Hence, the null hypothesis was rejected. It shows that rate of return on capital employed and C&AGs time lag are significantly related to each other.

(x) The effect of company characteristics with reporting time lag has been examined by testing the following null hypothesis:

(a) The coefficient of correlation between age of enterprise and reporting lag was negative 0.009. The computed value of 't' was found less than the tabular values. This shows the acceptance of null hypothesis that the age and reporting lag are not related to each other.

(b) The impact of gross turnover on reporting time lag has been evaluated by using 't' test. The computed value of 't' at 0.612 was less than the table values of 't'. The null hypothesis was accepted. It was found that gross turnover and reporting lag are not related to each other.

(c) The coefficient of correlation between size of enterprise and reporting lag was negative 0.174. The computed value of 't' was less than table values at 5% and 1% level of significance. This has shown that size of enterprise and reporting lag are not related to each other.

(d) The coefficient of correlation between rate of turnover and reporting lag was 0.012. It was evaluated by 't' test. The computed value of 't' is less than tabular values. Hence, the null hypothesis was accepted. It has shown that the rate of turnover and reporting lag are not related to each other.

(e) The influence of number of employees on reporting time lag was examined on 't' test. The computed value of 't' was less than tabular values. Thus, the null hypothesis was accepted. This has shown that number of employees and reporting lag are not related to each other.

(f) The impact of rate of return on reporting lag was examined by 't' test. The computed value is 1.059 at 9 degrees of freedom. The table values of 't' were more than computed value. It is found that rate of return and reporting lag are not related to each other.

5.1.3 Readability of Corporate Reports:

The effectiveness of a written communication largely depends upon the extent to which the receipient can read and understand the message. It also depends upon the writing skill and style of the writer. It can be improved by organisation of materials in fast moving and orderly form. Such arrangement creates interest and brings satisfaction to readers. In this sub section, the findings regarding readability are narrated briefly:

(i) The average readability score of 42.48 of the corporate reports indicates that the contents of the reports are fairly difficult to read and to understand by a common man. However, educated persons at the graduates level can easily read and understand the message. The readability score of individual corporate report in the selected MPSLPEs varies between 25.76 and 58.65. The standard deviation of 6.90 and coefficient of variation of 16.23 indicate wide variations in the readability of the report.

(ii) The average readability score of Directors' report of selected MPSLPEs is 41.57. If we measure this score at reading difficult level, it shows that the readability level is difficult and only a person of graduate level can read and understand the message easily. The readability score of the Directors' report varies between 24.19 and 60.59. The standard deviation of 9.15 and coefficient of variation of 22.01 shows wide variations in the readability level of the reports of the MPSLPEs.

(iii) The average readability score of auditors' report is 34.18. On the scale of difficult level and school grade level, it is measured as very difficult to read and understand. However the readability scores of audit reports varies between 11.17 to 65.65. The score has the standard deviation of 13.81 and coefficient of variation at 39.72. This indicates wide variations among the readability scores of the reports.

(iv) The average readability score of notes on account and foot notes is found 52.61. It shows a standard level of presentation and higher secondary school grade person can easily read and grasp the message. The readabilty score of notes on account and foot notes varies between 27.47 and 72.32. The standard deviation is 13.0 and coefficient of variation is 24.71. This has shown wide variations.

(v) The readability score of 77.77% of MPSLPEs have varied between 30% and 50%. This shows that the readability level of majority of annual reports is at difficult level. Only graduates and above can follow the message easily. Only 3 (16.67%) SLPEs' score has varied between 50% and 60% which are at standard readability level and higher secondary level person can read and understand the message easily. The readability score has not exceeded 60% This shows the greater scope of improvement.

(vi) Regarding Directors' report, the readability score of 65.33% of SLPEs was measured at difficult level. In case of one MPSLPE, a person having education upto high school can easily understand.

(vii) The readability score of audit report has varied between 10% and 70%. The 66% of MPSLPEs have readability score between 20% and 40%. The scope of simplication is much higher in this case.

viii) The readability of notes and notes on account has varied between 20 and 90. The difficulty level has gone up. Even a person with higher secondary can read and understand the message at lower level.

(ix) Effect of company characterstics on quality of readability of corporate annual report is found as follows:

(a) The coefficient of correlation between readability of annual report and age of the enterprise is 0.381. It was evaluated by 't' test. The computed value of 1.648 is less than the tabular values. This shows the acceptance of null hypothesis. It is found that the age of enterprise and readability of corporate report are not related to each other.

(b) The impact of gross turnover on readability of report was examined by finding the value of 'r' (- 0.300). It is found that the computed value of 't' is less than the tabular values. Hence, the null hypothesis was accepted. It is found that the gross turnover does not have significant influence on readability of annual reports.

(c) The null hypothesis between rate of return and readability was tested by 't' table. The computed value was less than the tabular values. The null hypothesis was accepted. It is found that both the factors are independant to each other.

(d) The value of 'r' between size of enterprise and readability of corporate report was negative at 0.124. It was evaluated on 't' scale. The computed value of 't' was found at 0.499. It was less than the table values of 2.731 at 5% and 2.947 at 1% levels of significance. This has shown the acceptance of null hypothesis. It indicates that size of enterprise does not influence the quality of readability of corporate reports.

(e) The null hypothesis between rate of turnover and quality of readability of reports was tested by 't' table. The computed value was less than tabular values. Hence, it is found that rate of turnover does not have significant/influence on readability of annual reports.

(f) The impact of number of employees on quality of readability of corporate report has been examined at 't' scale. It is found that the calculated value of 't' is 0.231 for 11 degrees of freedom. It was less than the tabular values. Hence, the null hyothesis was accepted. It is found that the number of employees in an enterprise does not have significant impact on quality of readability of corporate annual reports.

(x) The effect of company characteristics on the quality of readability of Directors report was examined by testing the following null hypothesis:

(a) The value of 'r' at 0.272 between the age of enterprise and readability scores of Directors' report was examined by 't' test. The computed value of 't' at 1.131 for 16 degrees of freedom was less than the tabulated values of 't' at 5% and 1% level of significance. This has shown the acceptance of null hypothesis. It was found that the age of enterprise does not have significant influence on quality of readability of Directors' report.

(b) The relationship between gross turnover and readability of directors report was tested on 't' scale. The calculated value of 't' was less than the tabular values at 5% and 1% level of significance. Thus, it was found that the gross turnover and quality of readability of Directors' report were not related to each other.

(c) The value of 'r' between rate of return on investment and readability score was tested by 't' table. The computed value is less than tabular values. Hence, the null hypothesis was accepted. It was found that the two variables are not related to each other.

(d) The value of 'r' was 0.520 between the size of enterprise and quality of readability of Directors' report. The computed value of 't' for 16 degrees of freedom was found at 2.435. It is more than the table values of 't' at both 5% and 1% level of significance. Thus, the null hypothesis was rejected. It was found that size of enterprise in terms of capital employed has significant influence on quality of readability of Directors' report. The larger PEs have better quality of readability of Directors' report than small enterprises.

(e) The impact of rate of turnover on readability of Directors' report was examined by 't' test. The computed value of 2.959 is greater than the tabular values of 2.731 at 5% level and 2.947 at 1% level of significance for 15 degrees of freedom. Hence, the null hypothesis was accepted. It was found that rate of turnover has significant influence on quality of readability of Directors' report.

(f) The impact of number of employees on readability of Directors' report was examined by 't' test. The computed value of 0.164 was much less than the tabular values. Thus, the null hypothesis was accepted. It was found that the number of employees does not have significant influence on readability scores of Directors' report.

(xi) The effect of company characteristics on readability of audit report has been evaluated by testing the following null hypothesis:

(a) The coefficient of correlation between age of enterprise and scores of readability of audit reports was negative 0.068. It was evaluated by 't' test. The computed value was less than the tabular values. Thus, it was found that the age of enterprise and quality of readability of audit report are not related to each other.

(b) The null hypothesis was tested to find the relationship between gross turnover and quality of readability of audit report. The computed values of 't' was 0.519. It was less than the tabular values. Thus, the null hypothesis is accepted. It shows that the two variables are not significantly related to each other.

(c) The coefficient of correlation between rate of return on investment and quality of readability of audit report was negative 0.409. It was evaluated by testing the null hypothesis. The computed value of 't' was less than the table values. Thus, the null hypothesis was accepted. The rate of return and quality of readability of audit report are not significantly related to each other.

(d) The co-efficient of correlation between size of enterprise and readability was negative (0.071). The computed value of 't'is (0.283). It is much less than table values of 't' at 5% and 1% levels for 16 degrees of freedom. This has shown the acceptance of null hypothesis. Thus, it was found that the size of enterprise and quality of audit report are not related to each other.

(e) The coefficient of correlation between rate of return and readability of audit report was 0.436. The calculated value of 't' was 1.875. It is less than the tabular values at both 5% and 1% levels of significance. Thus, the null hypothesis was accepted. It indicates that rate of return does not have significant influence on readability of audit report.

(f) The impact of size of employment on readability of audit report was evaluated by 't' test. The computed value of 2.005 was less than the table values at 5% and 1%. levels of significance. Thus, the null hypothesis was accepted. It has shown that the size of employment does not have significant influence on quality of readability of audit report.

(xii) The effect of company characteristics on readability of foot notes and notes on accounts have been examined by following null hypothesis:

(a) The coefficient of correlation between age and readability scores of foot notes and notes on account was 0.255. It was tested on 't' scale. The computed value of 't' is 1.004. It is less than the table values at 5% and 1% levels of significance. This shows the acceptance of null hypothesis. It indicates that the age and quality of readability of foot notes and notes of account are not significantly related to each other.

(b) The coefficient of correlation between gross turnover and quality of readability of notes and notes on account was negative 0.294. It was evaluated by using 't' test. The computed value of 't' was 1.233. It was less than the tabular values. Hence, the null hypothesis was accepted. It has shown that the gross turnover does not have significant influence on quality of readability of foot notes and notes on account.

(c) The relationship between rate of return and quality of readability of notes and notes on account was tested on 't' scale. The calculated value of 't' in respect of value of 'r' 0.369 was 1.122. It was less than the tabular values of 't' at 5% and 1% level of significance. Thus, it is found that the rate of return on investment does not have significant influence on quality of readability of foot notes and notes on account.

(d) The value of 'r' between size of enterprise and quality of readability was 0.175. The calculated value of `t' is less than the tabulated values. Therefore, the null hypothesis was accepted. It shows insignificant influence of the size of enterprise on quality of readability of notes.

(e) The impact of rate of turnover on quality of readability of foot notes and notes on accounts was tested by 't' test. The computed value of 't' was 1.145. It was found less than the table values at both 5% and 1% levels of significance. Hence, it is found that rate of turnover does not influence the quality of readability of foot notes and notes on account.

(f) The value of 'r' between number of employees and quality of readability of foot notes and notes on account was negative 0.149. It was evaluated by using 't' test. The calculated value of 't' at 0.152 was less than table values. Hence, the number of employees does not influence the quality of readability of foot notes and notes on account.

5.2 Suggestions:

The SLPEs in the state could not keep pace with rising public expectations in the sphere of corporate reporting practices. In some instances, they could not even meet bare minimum statutory requirements. The study itself has revealed the gaps in the sphere of extent of reporting, quantum of reporting, various time lags and readability aspects. A generalisation can be made that the management of these MPSLPEs has ignored the communication theory and its relevance to accounting and financial reporting. The study has clearly revealed that the management has ignored its social and statutory obligations regarding disclosure requirements. "What needs to be done to improve this state of affairs?" This question is before the all concerned i.e. the management of SLPEs , Bureau of State Level Public Enterprise, Professional bodies and State Government. From the study , an attempt has been made in this section to outline the various suggestions to tone-up the corporate reporting gaps in MPSLPEs .

5.2.1 Suggestions to Individual SLPE:

In this sub section, an attempt has been made to enlist various suggestions for individual SLPEs who are mainly affected by such problems.

(i) In case of MPS & FDC, the extent of disclosure is the lowest. The average score of 73.73% is beyond the reach of its individual score of 39.62%. In all the three segments also, this wide gap persists. There is a need to enhance the information level for this enterprise. When we look at the contents, the MPSLPEs have not shown the organisation structure, funds flow statement, ratios, highlights of the current year, future prospects and C&AGs report. If the management can look into these areas, the extent of disclosure will automatically improve.

(ii) In case of MPFDC, the time lag in terms of number of days is 2520. It is much more than the statutory allowed period of nine months. Much lag has been arisen on account of audit aspects. The audit time lag is 2291 days. This is much higher than the average time lag 1030 days. This clearly shows that the management has to be very careful about this aspect. In reporting lag also, the position of the enterprise is not comfortable. When look at the contents, we find that the areas like organisation structure, conservation of energy, ratios, pictorial presentation, etc. needs to strengthened.

(iii) In case of MPCSC,the readability score was the lowest at 25.76. This is much lower than the average readability score of 42.48 and the highest score of 58.65. The segments have also shown low scores (28.78 for Directors' report, 27.28 for Auditors' report and 36.27 for Foot notes and notes on accounts). The communication flow is to be strengthened. In case of reporting lag, the corporation should make efforts to reduce the lag from 97 days to around 40 to 50 days.

(iv) The readability score with respect to auditors' report is the lowest in case of MPEDC. It was recorded at 11.17 as compared to the average score of 34.78 and the highest score of 65.61. This score reveals that this report can be communicated to a few post graduates. On readability scale, this is termed as very difficult level. The management should make attempt to improve this readability by improving the quality of words used in the report. In case of C & AGs lag, it has the highest gap of 224 days. It is much higher than the average time lag of 80 days. This delay might have arisen because of the reluctance of management to give replies to audit objection within reasonable time. There is also much scope to improve its content specially with reference to Funds flow statement, ratios, Organisation structure, C & AGs' report, Accounting policies, Historical Summaries, etc. There is need to look into these aspects by the management of SLPEs so that the extent of disclosure may be strengthened.

5.2.2 Suggestion to SLPEs for the Aspects of Information Disclosure:

In this section, the suggestions to SLPEs were given for various aspects of corporate reporting practices.

(i) The emerging dimensions of disclosure practices have not at all been covered by the SLPEs. Social accounts, Current cost account, Human resource account, Value added statement, Cash flow statement, Statement of Profitability, Inflation accounting, Employees cost summaries, etc, were not at all shown in the corporate annual report of these SLPEs. The management of these SLPEs should develop a positive attitude towards the disclosure of these aspects.

(ii) The voluntary information disclosure level of MPSEDC, MPS & FDC, MPIDC, MPAIDC, MPSSIC, MPEDC, MPPHC, MPIC and MPTC is much lower than the average score of 40.25%. With the leaning of public enterprises towards the concept of social accountability, this gap needs to be filled up immediately.

(iii) In case of Directors' report, the contents of MPSEDC, MPS & FDC, MPAIDC, MPSSIC, MPEDC, MPPHC, MPSIC and MPCSC needs to be strengthened. This will improve the extent of information disclosure in Directors' report.

(iv) Even there are gaps in statutory disclosure of accounting information in the SLPEs; MPSEDC, MPS & FDC, MPAIDC, MPSSIC, MPEDC, MPSDC and MPTC have shown lesser disclosure level then the average disclosure levels of 83.51 percent. The management has to take care of this particular aspect as this involves the violation of statutory provisions.

(v) Audit time lag has delayed the release of annual reports of many SLPEs as compared to average audit lag of 1030 days. The crucial SLPEs in this sphere are MPAIDC (1589 days), MPFDC (2291 days), MPIDC (1706 days), MPSIC (1768 days) and MPTC (1944 days). The delay in finalisation of accounts on account of audit objections settlements needs to be minimised. This lag has caused the delay up to 6 years. If the reports are not being made available at the right time, the purpose of its beneficial use is lost.

(vi) The reporting lag is the time lag which is equal to the difference between the date of annual general meeting and the date of signature of C & AGs on the report. This time lag is crucial in case of MPFDC (229 days), MPIDC (233 days), MPSIC (151 days), MPLDC (295 days) and MPCSC (97 days). The management should identify the gaps in this area so that this time lag can also be reduced.

(vii) The readability score of the Directors' report of the following SLPEs is below average score of 41.57: MPSSIC (37.96), MPEDC (36.94), MPPHC (36.26), MPS & FDC (37.11), MPIDC (40.01), MPSIDC (36.69), MPFIDC (38.44), MPTC (39.53), MPBCC (28.78) and MPCSC (24.18). The average readability score of all the SLPEs is labelled as fairly difficult and can be understood by the graduates. A lot needs to be done so that this score may be put around sixty which is considered as standard readability level and can be understood by a user having higher secondary qualification.

(viii) In case of auditors' report, the average readability score was 34.78. The readability score of MPAIDC (32.27), MPLDC (33.65), MPTC (26.90), MPBCC (27.28), MPCSC (23.74), MPEB (30.25) and MPTDC (20.16) are to be improved to a satisfactory level of around 50.

(ix) The average readability score of foot notes and notes on account is 52.61. The management of following SLPEs have to take special measures to improve their readability position in this area - MPAIDC (43.30), MPPHC (44.27), MPS & FDC (51.50), MPFIDC (40.33), MPSEDC (52.38), MPBCC (36.27), MPCSC (27.47), MPEB (41.45) and MPTDC (35.54).

5.2.3 Suggestions to Bureau of State Enterprise Bhopal:

The Bureau acts as a nodal agency to co-ordinate and monitor the activities of all the SLPEs in the state. A more aggressive role is to be acquired by the Bureau to streamline the corporate reporting practices of these SLPEs. The following suggestions may be given in this regard:

(i) Regarding contents, the Bureau may suggest a format for all the SLPEs in the state. This will cover the disclosure requirements as per the Companies act and the accounting standards described by ICAI. The guidelines of the BPE shall also be taken into the account. The Bureau may take the help of professional bodies in preparing the format for corporate disclosures. The Bureau may also decide the desirability and extent of voluntary disclosure. In the light of public expectations, the Bureau may suggest the areas where such information disclosure is must.

(ii) Audit time lag is another crucial area where Bureau should take initiatives. A reporting cell in the Bureau will closely monitor the reporting process. The cell should give appropriate guidelines to regulate the delay with respect to finalisation of accounts, audit objection, convening of the annual general meeting, etc. If the Bureau insists for an interim report, the finalisation of accounts will be quicker.

(iii) It has been found that the readability scores of all the MPSLPEs is around 42.5. This score is considered as fairly difficult and only graduates can understand the message. The readability ease should be improved so that even a man with higher secondary qualification or secondary qualification can understood the message comfortably. The Bureau should suggest guidelines in this regard. The guidelines should suggest the type of phrases which are to be avoided in order to improve the readability ease.

(iv) Bureau should approach state government regarding a few statutory powers (if the SLPEs are flouting the guidelines of the Bureau). With the collected penalty amount, the Bureau may meet its establishment costs.

5.2.4 Suggestions to Professional Bodies:

The Professional bodies like ICAI, ICWAI, ICSI etc. have to play a pivotal role in promoting an effective mechanism of corporate reporting. The following suggestions deserve the special considerations by the professional bodies:

(i) ICAI has not set any standard specifically to suit the requirements of disclosures in SLPEs. AS-5 is of general nature. The peculiarities of a public sector enterprise needs to be taken care of. By way of appendix to AS-5,the disclosure requirement for a public enterprise be prepared and given specifically.

(ii) The professional bodies should help the Bureau in suggesting a format of annual report for SLPEs. This will improve interfirm comparision and the accounts department of concerned SLPE will have lesser burden in organising the contents of annual report. This will also reduce the delays.

(iii) ICSI should prepare a case to appoint company secretaries in all the SLPEs. This will regulate the procedural requirements of these corporate bodies. The annual general meeting will be convened in time and various time lags can be minimised with the Professional approach of company secretaries.

5.2.5 Suggestions to Government:

Government has got statutory and constitutional process to enforce its authority for the betterment of social.needs. It has to play a crucial role in improving the quantity of reporting practices in SLPEs. A few suggestions in this regard are as follows:

(i) At central level, Government should look at the provisions of the companies act. This should be examined with reference to various types of time lags reported in the MPSLPEs. The statutory period of nine months is flouted by the SLPEs as a rule. There is a need to make requisite ammendments in the act.

(ii) It has to confer a few powers to the Bureau for Co-ordinating and monitoring the reporting mechanism of these MPSLPEs. In that case, the government will not be over- burdened regarding the routines of disclosures of these MPSLPEs.

(iii) The Bureau be asked to present a report of discrepancies regarding the corporate disclosure annually. The Government may look into the discrepancies and pass necessary orders so that such discrepancies may not occur in future. The related secretarial work will be handled by the Bureau.

BIBLIOGRAPHY

A. Books

Agrawal, J.D. "*Accounting for Financial Analysis*", Indian Institute of Finance, Delhi, 1993.

Arunachalam.M.A.S., Raman K.S. "*Advanced Accountancy*" Himalaya Publishing House, Bombay, 1991.

Bhattacharya, H. "*How to Read a Balance Sheet*" Oxford & I.B.H. Publishing Co. Pvt. Ltd. New Delhi, 1991

Bhargava P. "*Companies Act. Law,, Practice & Precedents*" Taxman Alied Services, Delhi, 1990.

Charles T. Horngren, "*Management Accounting*" Prentice Hall, London 1984.

Chatterjee, B.K. "*Finance for non Finance Managers*" Jaico Publishing house, New Delhi 1991.

Claire Marston, "*Financial Reporting in India*", Crown Helm, London, 1986.

Dasgupta N. "*Financial Reporting in India*", Tiwari Publications, New Delhi, 1991.

———— "*Accounting standards: India and International*" Sultan chand & Sons Delhi, 1988.

David F.Hawkins "*Corporate Financial Reporting-Text and Cases*", Richard D. Irwin, Inc.Homewood, Illiois, 1988.

Horngren, C.T. & Suden, G.L. "*Introduction to Management Accounting*" Prentice-Hall of India Ltd. New Delhi 1990.

Jawahar Lal, "*Corporate Annual Reports-Theory and Practice*", Sterling Publishers, New Delhi, 1985.

Kapllan, R.S. and Atkinson,A.A. "*Advanced Management Accounting*" Prentice Hall of India Pvt. Ltd, New Delhi 1990.

Laxmi Narain, "*Principles and Practice of Public Enterprise Management*", Sultan Chand & Sons Ltd, Delhi, 1989.

Mishra R.K., Ravishankar S.& Nandagopal R. "*Management of State level Public Enterprises in India*", National Publishing House, New Delhi, 1989.

Porwal,L.S. "*Accounting Theory*", Tata Mc-Graw Hill, New Delhi. 1984.

Rao C.R. "*Balance Sheet - How 'True' and 'Fair'*". Brahmi Publishers, Bangalore, 1991.

Richard, M. Lynch, Robert, W. Williamson "*Accounting for Management: Planning and Control*" Tata Mc-Graw-Hill, New Delhi, 1989.

Richman, D.J. Thescon, M.H. Bovel C.L., Thill J.V."*Business Today*" Mc-Grow Publishing Co. New York, 1991.

Sharma R.C., "*Financial Reporting in Public Enterprises*", Tiwari Publications, New Delhi, 1991.

B. Articles and Research Papers

A.K. Basu, "Stock Market Efficiency And Corporate Financial Reporting" *Indian Journal of Accounting*, vol-xix. June 1989.

B.B. Pradhan,"An Analysis on timeliness of Annual Report" *Finance India*, vol-III No.1 March 1989.

——————"Corporate Reporting In India: A Historical Perspective" *Finance India*, Vol-III No.IV Dec.1989.

D.K. Chakraborty, "Public Sector Enterprises and Corporate Reporting in India" *Indian Journal of accounting in India,* Vol XIX, June 1989, Pt-I

Henry, Reiling and John C, Burton, "Financial Statements: Signposts as well as Milestones" *Harward Business Review, Control series Pt-III.*

L.S. Porwal,"Standard Setting for Corporate Financial Accounting and Reporting in India" The "*Management Accountant*" Vol-24 No.-9 SEP,1989,

Narendra P. Sarda, "Corporate Reporting "*Chartered Accountant*", Vol-XXXVIII, No.1 July 1990.

R. Devarajan, "Corporate Reporting Practices in India: Concepts and Current Issues" *Chartered Accountant*, June 1991.

Satish Chandra, "Corporate Social Reporting: A case study of SAIL "*The Journal of Institute of Public enterprises*, Vol - 14 June 1991 No.2

Umesh Holaw, Corporate Reporting and Financial Analysis" *Accounting and Finance* **Vol-VI No.1 Spring, 1992.**

Walter F. Frense & Robert K, Mautz, "Financial Reporting by Whom? "*Harvard Business Review Control Series Pt-III.*

INDEX